Quality
2/17/11
95

W9-CPB-910

War Crimes

Other Books of Related Interest:

Opposing Viewpoints Series

The Armed Forces

Biological Warfare

At Issue Series

Biological and Chemical Weapons

Is Torture Ever Justified?

Military Recruiters

Current Controversies Series

The Arms Trade

Homeland Security

"Congress shall make
no law . . . abridging
the freedom of speech,
or of the press."

First Amendment to the U.S. Constitution

The basic foundation of our democracy is the First Amendment guarantee of freedom of expression. The Opposing Viewpoints Series is dedicated to the concept of this basic freedom and the idea that it is more important to practice it than to enshrine it.

OPPOSING
VIEWPOINTS®
SERIES

War Crimes

Margaret Haerens, Book Editor

GREENHAVEN PRESS
A part of Gale, Cengage Learning

GALE
CENGAGE Learning

Detroit • New York • San Francisco • New Haven, Conn • Waterville, Maine • London

Christine Nasso, *Publisher*
Elizabeth Des Chenes, *Managing Editor*

© 2011 Greenhaven Press, a part of Gale, Cengage Learning

Gale and Greenhaven Press are registered trademarks used herein under license.

For more information, contact:
Greenhaven Press
27500 Drake Rd.
Farmington Hills, MI 48331-3535
Or you can visit our Internet site at gale.cengage.com

For product information and technology assistance, contact us at

Gale Customer Support, 1-800-877-4253
For permission to use material from this text or product, submit all requests online at www.cengage.com/permissions

Further permissions questions can be emailed to permissionrequest@cengage.com

Articles in Greenhaven Press anthologies are often edited for length to meet page requirements. In addition, original titles of these works are changed to clearly present the main thesis and to explicitly indicate the author's opinion. Every effort is made to ensure that Greenhaven Press accurately reflects the original intent of the authors. Every effort has been made to trace the owners of copyrighted material.

Cover image © iStockPhoto.com/Andrejs Zemdega.

LIBRARY OF CONGRESS CATALOGING-IN-PUBLICATION DATA

War crimes / Margaret Haerens, book editor.
    p. cm. -- (Opposing viewpoints)
    Includes bibliographical references and index.
    ISBN 978-0-7377-4996-0 (hardcover) -- ISBN 978-0-7377-4997-7 (pbk.)
    1. War crimes--Juvenile literature. I. Haerens, Margaret.
    K5301.W3673 2010
    341.6'9--dc22

                                                                    2010022995

Printed in the United States of America
1 2 3 4 5 6 7 14 13 12 11 10

Contents

Chapter 4: What Governments and Individuals Should Be Tried for War Crimes?

Why Consider
Opposing Viewpoints?

> "*The only way in which a human being can make some approach to knowing the whole of a subject is by hearing what can be said about it by persons of every variety of opinion and studying all modes in which it can be looked at by every character of mind. No wise man ever acquired his wisdom in any mode but this.*"
>
> John Stuart Mill

In our media-intensive culture it is not difficult to find differing opinions. Thousands of newspapers and magazines and dozens of radio and television talk shows resound with differing points of view. The difficulty lies in deciding which opinion to agree with and which "experts" seem the most credible. The more inundated we become with differing opinions and claims, the more essential it is to hone critical reading and thinking skills to evaluate these ideas. Opposing Viewpoints books address this problem directly by presenting stimulating debates that can be used to enhance and teach these skills. The varied opinions contained in each book examine many different aspects of a single issue. While examining these conveniently edited opposing views, readers can develop critical thinking skills such as the ability to compare and contrast authors' credibility, facts, argumentation styles, use of persuasive techniques, and other stylistic tools. In short, the Opposing Viewpoints Series is an ideal way to attain the higher-level thinking and reading skills so essential in a culture of diverse and contradictory opinions.

In addition to providing a tool for critical thinking, Opposing Viewpoints books challenge readers to question their own strongly held opinions and assumptions. Most people form their opinions on the basis of upbringing, peer pressure, and personal, cultural, or professional bias. By reading carefully balanced opposing views, readers must directly confront new ideas as well as the opinions of those with whom they disagree. This is not to simplistically argue that everyone who reads opposing views will—or should—change his or her opinion. Instead, the series enhances readers' understanding of their own views by encouraging confrontation with opposing ideas. Careful examination of others' views can lead to the readers' understanding of the logical inconsistencies in their own opinions, perspective on why they hold an opinion, and the consideration of the possibility that their opinion requires further evaluation.

Evaluating Other Opinions

To ensure that this type of examination occurs, Opposing Viewpoints books present all types of opinions. Prominent spokespeople on different sides of each issue as well as well-known professionals from many disciplines challenge the reader. An additional goal of the series is to provide a forum for other, less known, or even unpopular viewpoints. The opinion of an ordinary person who has had to make the decision to cut off life support from a terminally ill relative, for example, may be just as valuable and provide just as much insight as a medical ethicist's professional opinion. The editors have two additional purposes in including these less known views. One, the editors encourage readers to respect others' opinions—even when not enhanced by professional credibility. It is only by reading or listening to and objectively evaluating others' ideas that one can determine whether they are worthy of consideration. Two, the inclusion of such viewpoints encourages the important critical thinking skill of objectively evaluating an author's credentials and bias. This evaluation will illuminate an author's reasons for taking a particular stance on an issue and will aid in readers' evaluation of the author's ideas.

It is our hope that these books will give readers a deeper understanding of the issues debated and an appreciation of the complexity of even seemingly simple issues when good and honest people disagree. This awareness is particularly important in a democratic society such as ours in which people enter into public debate to determine the common good. Those with whom one disagrees should not be regarded as enemies but rather as people whose views deserve careful examination and may shed light on one's own.

Thomas Jefferson once said that "difference of opinion leads to inquiry, and inquiry to truth." Jefferson, a broadly educated man, argued that "if a nation expects to be ignorant and free . . . it expects what never was and never will be." As individuals and as a nation, it is imperative that we consider the opinions of others and examine them with skill and discernment. The Opposing Viewpoints Series is intended to help readers achieve this goal.

David L. Bender and Bruno Leone,
Founders

Introduction

"You will be judged in years to come by how you responded to genocide on your watch."

—*Nicholas Kristof,*
American journalist

On October 26, 2005, Iranian president Mahmoud Ahmadinejad gave a speech at the "World Without Zionism" conference in Tehran, Iran. The Iranian leader's words that day garnered worldwide controversy for his incendiary comments about Israel. According to a full transcript of the speech published in the *New York Times* on October 30, Ahmadinejad agreed with Ayatollah Khomeini's statement that Israel's "occupying regime must be wiped off the map for great justice." He concluded, "I have no doubt that the new wave that has started in Palestine, and we witness it in the Islamic world too, will eliminate this disgraceful stain from the Islamic world." Although there have been different translations of Ahmadinejad's remarks that day, many experts interpret the Iranian leader's words as a threat to the Israeli government and a direct and public incitement to commit genocide against the Jewish people.

When Ahmadinejad's remarks were published in newspapers around the world in subsequent days, a firestorm of world opinion erupted. Israeli vice premier Shimon Peres called for the expulsion of Iran from the United Nations (UN). "Since the United Nations was established in 1945, there has never been a head of state that is a UN member state that publicly called for the elimination of another UN member state," Peres told Israel Radio a few days after the speech. Other world leaders stood up against the perceived threat in

Ahmadinejad's words. Canada's prime minister Paul Martin stated that "this threat to Israel's existence, this call for genocide coupled with Iran's obvious nuclear ambitions is a matter that the world cannot ignore." In 2008 British prime minister Gordon Brown commented that "to those who believe that threatening statements fall upon indifferent ears we say in one voice—it is totally abhorrent for the president of Iran to call for Israel to be wiped from the map of the world." UN secretary-general Kofi Annan expressed dismay at the comments and reminded all member states that Israel is a long-standing United Nations member "with the same rights and obligations as every other member."

Although Ahmadinejad later stated that his speech had been misinterpreted, world leaders were alarmed at the perceived threat to Israel and looked for ways to prosecute him. In 2006 calls for the Iranian leader to be tried for inciting genocide, which is a war crime, were raised by prominent world diplomats and officials. One of the loudest voices was the United States' UN ambassador John Bolton. "It's important that if we are in this stage where we're being given early warning, unambiguously, on what his intentions are, then it's time to take action," Bolton told a Conference of Presidents of Major American Jewish Organizations symposium. Future Australian prime minister Kevin Rudd asserted that Ahmadinejad should be brought before the International Criminal Court (ICC) on charges of incitement to genocide for those statements and others regarding Israel under the UN's Convention on the Prevention and Punishment of the Crime of Genocide.

As calls for indictment got stronger, Iranian leaders and journalists argued that world reaction was discriminatory and politically motivated. Ali Ahani, the Iranian ambassador to the European Union, maintained that the world ignored Israeli violence and threats while focusing exclusively on Ahmadinejad and other Arab leaders. They argued that two standards existed: one for Arab countries and another for Israel. Other Iranian leaders charged Western political figures with overreacting to smear Iran's international standing.

The controversy over Ahmadinejad's remarks and possible indictment reflects the problems the ICC has encountered in other situations, such as in the Sudan. Calls for the involvement of the ICC to investigate war crimes, genocide, and incitement to genocide are quickly countered by charges of politically motivated actions and discrimination. The ICC is accused of being a tool of the Western powers, or of Israel or the United States, while oppressing certain Arab or African countries. Some countries are accused of meddling in the process and refusing to join the ICC so they can claim that the international court has no jurisdiction over their citizens.

The United States is one of these countries. While the United States has been vocal about its concerns over the ICC— particularly that the ICC would interfere with national sovereignty and security—it has been willing to limitedly engage the ICC on matters it deems within its interests. Critics view this self-interested approach as problematic and encourage the United States to fully engage the ICC.

The authors of the viewpoints presented in *Opposing Viewpoints: War Crimes* explore many of these issues and other challenges facing the world community in the following chapters: Who Can Be Considered War Criminals? How Should the United States Address War Crimes? How Should the United States Deal with the ICC? and What Governments and Individuals Should Be Tried for War Crimes? The information in this volume will provide insight into the relationship between the United States and the ICC as well as the issues surrounding the prevention, investigation, and prosecution of governments and individuals accused of war crimes, genocide, inciting genocide, and crimes against humanity.

OPPOSING VIEWPOINTS® SERIES

CHAPTER 1

Who Can Be Considered War Criminals?

Chapter Preface

On April 8, 2008, a U.S. cargo ship, the *Maersk Alabama*, bound for Mombasa, Kenya, with seventeen thousand metric tons of cargo was hijacked by four well-armed Somali pirates off the southeast Somali coast. The crew, composed of twenty seasoned sailors, was prepared for such an event. Somali pirates had roamed the coasts since the early twenty-first century, leading to hundreds of millions of dollars in ransom demands. The American crew had received some anti-piracy training, and crew members quickly locked themselves in the engine room. After arming themselves and planning their counterattack, the crew launched its plans and regained control of the ship. After more fighting, however, the pirates captured the captain of the ship, Richard Phillips. Realizing that they wouldn't be able to keep control, the pirates fled on a large lifeboat with food and their American hostage. It was later reported that their intentions were to wait for more pirates and resources to hijack the cargo-rich U.S. ship.

The next day, the U.S. destroyer USS *Bainbridge* arrived on the scene to aid the *Maersk Alabama*. The destroyer quickly tracked down the lifeboat with the pirates and their hostage onboard but kept its distance. Although the two vessels established radio communication, no progress was made in getting the pirates to release the American captain. When one of the pirates left the lifeboat to board the USS *Bainbridge* to negotiate a ransom for the captive, the situation quickly deteriorated. Determining that Captain Phillips's life was in imminent danger, U.S. Navy SEAL snipers killed the remaining three Somali pirates on the lifeboat and rescued the hostage.

Months later history repeated itself. In November 2009 the *Maersk Alabama* suffered another attack by Somali pirates as it carried cargo to Mombasa, Kenya. This time, however, the hijacking attempt was repelled by a private security team hired to protect the ship, its crew, and its cargo.

With Somali piracy in the busy region an increasing and costly problem, a debate about how to classify captured pirates has risen. Many observers contend that the U.S. government should treat the pirates as war criminals who have committed crimes against mankind. Other commentators argue that the Somali pirates are motivated by money—not ideology or political concerns—and therefore should be treated as felons and tried in the American legal system.

The debate over the treatment of Somali pirates echoes some of the other issues in this chapter, which focuses on the question of what constitutes a war criminal. Other viewpoints in the chapter explore whether private security firms, terrorists, and groups that use mass rape should be considered war criminals.

"Treating an al Qaeda operative who enters the United States to carry out an attack as a common criminal not only denies the nature of this challenge we face, but it works to level the playing field to our disadvantage."

Terrorists Should Be Classified as War Criminals and Enemy Combatants

David B. Rivkin Jr. and Lee A. Casey

David B. Rivkin Jr. and Lee A. Casey are lawyers and former U.S. Department of Justice officials. In the following viewpoint, they argue that it is consistent with law, morality, and history to treat captured enemy personnel as enemy combatants or war criminals. Treating terrorists as regular criminals, they conclude, only serves to deny the threat that terrorism poses to the United States.

As you read, consider the following questions:

1. How does Michael Kinsley defend treating Umar Farouk Abdulmutallab as a criminal defendant?

2. Why do the authors believe that choosing the U.S. border as a dividing line is incorrect?

3. According to the authors, why don't law enforcement and war mix well?

Writing in the *New York Times*, Michael Kinsley defends treating Umar Farouk Abdulmutallab (the al Qaeda operative who recently tried to blow up an airliner over Detroit [in Dec. 2009]) as a criminal defendant rather than an enemy combatant. He argues that, since any line to be drawn between waging war and engaging the criminal-justice system is going to be arbitrary, the U.S. border is as good a line as any. That is, al Qaeda terrorists captured abroad are enemy combatants while those captured at home are criminal defendants, entitled to all the rights provided by our Constitution and statutes.

The problem is that the lines between law enforcement and war are not arbitrary (but rather well defined by law and tradition) and that choosing the U.S. border as a nice, bright line is not driven by military strategy, logic, or law. There is nothing sacred about American territory. Indeed, at least two major wars—the Revolutionary War and Civil War—and numerous military conflicts with Indian tribes were prosecuted on American soil. This war can be (and has been) fought here as well as in Afghanistan, Iraq, or Yemen. In fact, the United States is the enemy's favored battleground, because this is where al Qaeda's most desired targets—American civilians—are most heavily concentrated. This is why the victims of 9/11 [the terrorist attacks of Sept. 11, 2001] died in New York, Washington, and the fields of Pennsylvania, rather than at American facilities and installations abroad.

Drawing the Line

Nor, in fact, is the line Mr. Kinsley proposes arbitrary; it is ideological. Adopting a war-abroad/law-enforcement-at-home rule is nothing but an exercise in political triangulation. It indulges the Left's fundamental disdain for the use of military force, while permitting the [Barack] Obama administration to claim that it actually is trying to protect the American people by taking the fight to the enemy. Read between the lines—or read the lines. Mr. Kinsley contrasts our roles "as a liberal democracy and as a legitimately aggrieved superpower." Why is it, exactly, that those two things are inconsistent? We are, in fact, a legitimately aggrieved liberal democracy that happens, also, to be a superpower.

At bottom, law enforcement and war do not mix well because they begin with very different assumptions and, as a result, are governed by fundamentally different rule sets. It is those assumptions that the Obama administration and the Left in general find problematic. Thus, our civilian criminal-justice system is designed to constrain the overwhelming power of the state vis-à-vis an individual criminal defendant. Ask any criminal-defense lawyer: The prosecution has the edge at almost every point. It decides who to investigate and who to charge, has resources that (however constrained) far outweigh those of any ordinary defendant, and controls the evidence, crime scene, and witnesses.

Presented with these realities, our body polity has decided at least since the 1960s to temper and handicap the government's ability to investigate, prosecute, and punish criminal misconduct. This is why, as Mr. Kinsley correctly describes, many a murderer, rapist, or child molester goes free. To be sure, despite all of these constraints on the police, prosecutors, and prison authorities, in the final analysis, the state is overwhelmingly powerful as compared with even the most deviant and potent criminals. This is true even in cases of organized crime and drug gangs. However well armed and ruthless such groups may be, any properly functioning state will be capable of marshalling sufficient force to maintain an overwhelming predominance.

Facing the Challenge of Terrorism

In war, the challenge to governmental authority is not individual but collective, and is far more dangerous as a result. Foreign belligerents have broader means and a stronger motive to disrupt the social order than common criminals do. The power of their armaments and the pervasiveness of their ideology can often be traced to the direct or indirect support they receive from other international players. All states at some basic level have an interest in maintaining civil law and order—and however much foreign police or judicial systems may hamper U.S. law enforcement in certain cases, they do not actively seek to promote the criminal activity involved. By contrast, in war, foreign states may choose to support—directly or indirectly—enemy belligerents, effectively augmenting their reach and capabilities.

As a result, governmental power is necessarily augmented during wartime. This is especially the case in liberal-democratic states, where that power is ordinarily subject to greater limits than in authoritarian regimes. It is, of course, this very augmentation that the [George W.] Bush administration's critics found so unacceptable after Sept. 11, 2001. The alternative, however, is accepting greater risk to the civilians al Qaeda wants to target. The right way to proceed, consistent with the law, morality, and history, is to treat captured enemy personnel as enemy combatants, subject to the laws of war. By contrast, criminals—including individuals who commit terrorist acts but, whatever their ideological predilections, are not members of entities such as al Qaeda that have been engaged in an armed conflict with us (this would include [Oklahoma federal building bomber] Timothy McVeigh and [Fort Hood shooting suspect] Major Nidal Malik Hasan)—should be treated as criminal suspects subject to the workings of the criminal-justice system. Treating an al Qaeda operative who enters the United States to carry out an attack as a common criminal not only denies the nature of this challenge we face, but it works to level the playing field to our disadvantage.

> "Labeling its members as combatants el-
> evates its cause and gives al Qaeda an
> undeserved status."

Terrorists Should Be Classified as Criminals Subject to Criminal Prosecution

Wesley K. Clark and Kal Raustiala

Wesley K. Clark is a fellow at the Burkle Center for International Relations at the University of California, Los Angeles (UCLA). Kal Raustiala is the director of the Burkle Center and a law professor at UCLA. In the following viewpoint, they contend that classifying terrorists as enemy combatants provides them legitimacy and, in the process, endangers U.S. traditions. They conclude that terrorists should be treated as criminals who are subject to criminal courts.

As you read, consider the following questions:

1. How did a federal appeals court in Richmond, Virginia, rule on the indefinite detention of Ali al-Marri in 2007?

2. How are the traditional categories of combatant and civilian muddled in the war on terror, according to the authors?

3. How do the authors believe the United States should treat Ali al-Marri?

The line between soldier and civilian has long been central to the law of war. Today that line is being blurred in the struggle against transnational terrorists. Since 9/11, the Bush administration has sought to categorize members of al Qaeda and other jihadists as "unlawful combatants" rather than treat them as criminals.

The federal courts are increasingly wary of this approach, and rightly so. In a stinging rebuke, this summer a federal appeals court in Richmond, Va., struck down the government's indefinite detention of a civilian, Ali al-Marri, by the military. The case illustrates once again the pitfalls of our current approach.

Don't Give Terrorists Legitimacy

Treating terrorists as combatants is a mistake for two reasons. First, it dignifies criminality by according terrorist killers the status of soldiers. Under the law of war, military service members receive several privileges. They are permitted to kill the enemy and are immune from prosecution for doing so. They must, however, carefully distinguish between combatant and civilian and ensure that harm to civilians is limited.

Critics have rightly pointed out that traditional categories of combatant and civilian are muddled in a struggle against terrorists. In a traditional war, combatants and civilians are relatively easy to distinguish. The 9/11 hijackers, by contrast, dressed in ordinary clothes and hid their weapons. They acted not as citizens of Saudi Arabia, an ally of America, but as members of al Qaeda, a shadowy transnational network. And their prime targets were innocent civilians.

By treating such terrorists as combatants, however, we accord them a mark of respect and dignify their acts. And we undercut our own efforts against them in the process. Al Qaeda represents no state, nor does it carry out any of a state's responsibilities for the welfare of its citizens. Labeling its members as combatants elevates its cause and gives al Qaeda an undeserved status.

Fight Terrorism with Law Enforcement

If we are to defeat terrorists across the globe, we must do everything possible to deny legitimacy to their aims and means, and gain legitimacy for ourselves. As a result, terrorism should be fought first with information exchanges and law enforcement, then with more effective domestic security measures. Only as a last resort should we call on the military and label such activities "war." The formula for defeating terrorism is well known and time-proven.

Labeling terrorists as combatants also leads to this paradox: While the deliberate killing of civilians is never permitted in war, it is legal to target a military installation or asset. Thus the attack by al Qaeda on the destroyer *Cole* in Yemen in 2000 would be allowed, as well as attacks on command and control centers like the Pentagon. For all these reasons, the more appropriate designation for terrorists is not "unlawful combatant" but the one long used by the United States: criminal.

America Must Be Beacon

The second major problem with the approach of the Bush administration is that it endangers our political traditions and our commitment to liberty, and further damages America's legitimacy in the eyes of others. Almost 50 years ago, at the height of the cold war, the Supreme Court reaffirmed the "deeply rooted and ancient opposition in this country to the extension of military control over civilians."

A great danger in treating operatives for al Qaeda as combatants is precisely that its members are not easily distinguished from the population at large. The government wields frightening power when it can designate who is, and who is not, subject to indefinite military detention. The Marri case turned on this issue. Mr. Marri is a legal resident of the United States and a citizen of Qatar; the government contends that he is a sleeper agent of al Qaeda. For the last four years he has been held as an enemy combatant at the Navy brig in Charleston, S.C.

The federal court held that while the government can arrest and convict civilians, under current law the military cannot seize and detain Mr. Marri. Nor would it necessarily be constitutional to do so, even if Congress expressly authorized the military detention of civilians. At the core of the court's reasoning is the belief that civilians and combatants are distinct. Had Ali al-Marri fought for an enemy nation, military detention would clearly be proper. But because he is accused of being a member of al Qaeda, and is a citizen of a friendly nation, he should not be treated as a warrior.

Treat Terrorists Like Criminals

Cases like this illustrate that in the years since 9/11, the Bush administration's approach to terrorism has created more problems than it has solved. We need to recognize that terrorists, while dangerous, are more like modern-day pirates than warriors. They ought to be pursued, tried and convicted in the courts. At the extreme, yes, military force may be required. But the terrorists themselves are not "combatants." They are merely criminals, albeit criminals of an especially heinous type, and that label suggests the appropriate venue for dealing with the threats they pose.

We train our soldiers to respect the line between combatant and civilian. Our political leaders must also respect this distinction, lest we unwittingly endanger the values for which we are fighting, and further compromise our efforts to strengthen our security.

> *"Today most private security contractors operate in an environment where systems of criminal accountability are rarely used."*

Private Security Firms in Iraq Can Be Tried as War Criminals

Human Rights First

Human Rights First is a nonprofit, human rights organization. In the following viewpoint, the organization asserts that private security contractors (PSCs) are able to operate in Iraq and Afghanistan without any accountability, which has resulted in tragedy. They argue that PSCs must be held accountable or their actions may imperil American efforts in both countries and throughout the world.

As you read, consider the following questions:

1. According to government estimates, how many private contractors are operating in Iraq?

2. Who has more forces in Iraq: the U.S. military or private companies?

3. How many PSCs are estimated to be in Iraq, according to Human Rights First?

On September 16, 2007, private security contractors (PSCs) working for Blackwater Worldwide were running an armed convoy through Baghdad. Iraqi government officials charge that these Blackwater contractors, with no justification, killed 17 civilians and wounded 24 more in the Nisoor Square neighborhood of Baghdad. The incident created a political firestorm in Iraq, the United States, and around the world. Although the facts are still under investigation, the incident brought intensive focus to the role of PSCs operating in Iraq.

The U.S. government's reaction to the shootings at Nisoor Square has been characterized by confusion, defensiveness, a multiplicity of uncoordinated *ad hoc* investigations, and interagency finger-pointing. These failures underscored the Justice Department's (DOJ's) unwillingness or inability to systematically investigate and prosecute allegations of serious violent crimes.

Americans Are Also Victims

And these failures even extend to cases where U.S. citizens have been victims, such as the alleged 2005 gang rape of Jamie Leigh Jones by coworkers at a forward operating base in Iraq. At the time Jones worked for Kellogg Brown & Root (KBR), Inc. (then a Halliburton subsidiary). She has now filed a civil law suit against KBR, the U.S. government, and others. Justice Department officials in Iraq were briefed on the incident at the time, but DOJ declined even to open an investigation for more than two years, and they did so only when facing the prospect of embarrassing publicity relating to the case. There still has been no prosecution of her assailants. There has been a similar failure to investigate and prosecute private contractors involved in the abuses at Abu Ghraib prison during 2003. The images of Army Specialists Lynndie England and Charles

Graner are imprinted in the public memory of that scandal—in large part because of their military court-martial prosecutions. By contrast, the role of private contractors at Abu Ghraib has received little public attention. Several contractors were there and participated in the interrogations at Abu Ghraib, including "Big Steve"—Steven Stefanowicz, a private contractor interrogator employed by CACI International, Inc., on a Department of the Interior contract—and several other CACI and L3 Communications Titan Group (then its own entity, Titan) contractors. But the role of these contractors has never been fully investigated by the Justice Department. While 11 soldiers from Abu Ghraib were convicted on charges related to detainee abuse there, not one CACI or Titan civilian contractor has ever even been *charged* with a crime. Formal Army investigative reports identified at least five private contractors as implicated in serious crimes at Abu Ghraib. These Army investigators found evidence that some private contractors even gave direction and orders to soldiers who were prosecuted. Cases examined by the Army's Criminal Investigation Division (CID) [formally known as the United States Army Criminal Investigation Command (USACIDC)] were referred to DOJ within months after these revelations. Yet in the more than three years since then, the Justice Department—specifically, the U.S. Attorney's Office for the Eastern District of Virginia—has failed to prosecute any of these private contractors.

Documented Cases of Sexual Abuse

These incidents are the tip of the iceberg. Over the last several years there have been scores of reports of serious abuse by private contractors in Iraq and Afghanistan—both in the context of interrogations and in the use of excessive and often lethal force in various security operations. Many of these incidents have been well documented. Through February 2006 only 20 cases of alleged detainee abuse involving contractors are known to have been referred to DOJ. Nisoor Square and the Christmas Eve Baghdad shooting are the only known cases of security contractor abuse against local nationals that have been referred to DOJ. And only one civilian contractor, David Passaro, has ever been prosecuted by the U.S. government for violence towards local nationals. Passaro was a Central Intelligence Agency (CIA) contractor at a U.S. Army base in Afghanistan. In June 2003 Passaro beat a local Afghani named Abdul Wali in the course of a two-day "interrogation." Wali died in custody the next day. Passaro was tried in August 2006, convicted of multiple assault charges, and sentenced to more than eight years in prison.

Based on data reported by the Department of Defense (DOD) and Department of State . . . , estimates show that there are now approximately 180,000 private contractors operating in Iraq today—more than the number of U.S. military forces there. The U.S. government has neither asserted sufficient control over the situation nor even provided comprehensive information on how many private security contractors work there. Officials at both DOD and [the State Department] cannot provide the number of private security and other contractors *funded by the U.S. government* currently in Iraq.

PSCs in Iraq

But we do know that significant numbers of these contractors—tens of thousands of them—are armed and carrying out military-style security functions, working for several U.S. government agencies. Human Rights First estimates there are at least 35,000 PSCs in Iraq today. Collectively, PSCs comprise the second-largest armed security force in the "coalition of the willing" in Iraq, second only to the U.S. military. They represent a larger force even than the *combined* forces of all of the coalition nations in Iraq other than the United States.

Most private security contractors in Iraq are Iraqi nationals, but thousands—perhaps tens of thousands—are U.S. and "third country" nationals. These contractors work for more than 180 companies, including Aegis Defense Services [Limited], DynCorp International, the Centurion Group, Control Risks Group, Erinys, MPRI, Triple Canopy and Blackwater Worldwide, to cite a few of the major players. While most individual contractors providing security services undoubtedly abide by the law and carry out their functions in a professional manner, there is a widespread and disturbing pattern of illegality and misconduct by private security contractors in these operations.

Consider these cases:

Zapata. On May 28, 2005, U.S. Marines detained contractors from the American company Zapata Engineering, accusing the contractors of "repeatedly firing weapons at civilians and Marines, erratic driving, and possession of illegal weapons," and posing a "direct threat to Marine personnel." Although 16 American contractors lost their jobs with Zapata and were banned from working in the Marine sector of Iraq, none of them was ever prosecuted.

Triple Canopy. On July 8, 2006, Triple Canopy security contractors reportedly fired upon Iraqi civilian vehicles, damaging two vehicles and possibly causing casualties. Three members of the team described at least one of the incidents as unwarranted and admitted there was no threat, and the fourth team member—the alleged shooter—was accused by his teammates of saying he wanted "to kill somebody today" before starting the mission. But these shootings came to public attention only through a wrongful termination suit later filed by two of the fired Triple Canopy guards; the U.S. government seems never to have conducted a criminal investigation into the incidents. Triple Canopy fired the three American members of the team, two of which claim they were fired in retaliation for their reporting of the incident.

Blackwater 2006. On Christmas Eve 2006, Andrew Moonen, a Blackwater contractor, allegedly shot and killed Raheem

Khalif Hulaichi in Baghdad's International Zone. Hulaichi was a member of Iraqi Vice President Adil Abdul-Mahdi's security detail. According to a CID report, after drinking heavily at a Christmas party, Moonen passed through a gate near the Iraqi prime minister's compound and, when confronted by Hulaichi, fired repeatedly with his Glock 9mm pistol, hitting the guard three times, then fled the scene. Hulaichi died soon after. With State Department facilitation, Blackwater hurried Moonen out of Iraq. Now more than a year later, the FBI [Federal Bureau of Investigation] and the Justice Department's U.S. Attorney's Office for the Western District of Washington reportedly are still investigating the case, although the office declined to confirm this to Human Rights First. Shortly after the incident, Mr. Moonen found work with another contractor, Combat Support Associates (CSA), which provides logistics support to U.S. troops in Kuwait under a DOD contract. A CSA spokesman stated that nothing "untoward" was found in Moonen's record during the standard background review conducted of all prospective employees. To date no one has been charged or prosecuted in Hulaichi's killing.

Human Rights First estimates that there are thousands of occasions in Iraq in which PSCs have discharged their weapons, hundreds of times toward civilians. But because of lax reporting requirements, inadequate supervision and the near-complete failure—primarily of DOJ—to investigate incidents, it is impossible to determine how many civilians were killed or wounded in these incidents. Clearly much more must be done to ensure this unacceptable situation does not continue.

Inadequate Efforts and Resources

The existing legal framework for holding private security contractors criminally accountable is based on a patchwork of federal statutes that provide a piecemeal approach to criminal jurisdiction. But together these laws do provide extensive—

Private Security Contractors: A Definition

There is no universal, agreed definition of the term "private security contractor." Other terms used in the industry, the literature, and by other observers include "private military contractors" and, most pejoratively, "mercenaries." Some companies in the PSC industry—and it most certainly *is* an industry—identify themselves as PSCs, but no serious analysis can turn on company self-identification. Human Rights First uses here an essentially functional definition of the term in light of the actual activities of such contractors fielded in Iraq and Afghanistan with a basic *security* mission—that is, a core mission to protect people (other than themselves) or things, to include guarding government (and contractors') facilities, protecting government personnel (and other government contractors) and United Nations (UN) and other international organization staff as well, and providing security for convoys. While in other contexts PSCs may perform some or all of their functions unarmed, in Iraq and Afghanistan they almost invariably carry weapons.

Human Rights First,
Private Security Contractors at War:
Ending the Culture of Impunity. *New York:*
Human Rights First, 2008. www.humanrightsfirst.org.

although imperfect—coverage. If used these laws would cover most of the serious violent crimes committed by contractors in Iraq and Afghanistan. By law, authority to prosecute these cases is shared by the Justice and Defense Departments. In practice, however, *neither* of these federal agencies is aggressively investigating nor prosecuting contractors. The U.S. government has not devoted adequate effort or resources to carry out the necessary criminal investigations or prosecutions.

The Justice Department bears primary responsibility for this inaction. Today most private security contractors operate in an environment where systems of criminal accountability are rarely used. This has created a culture of impunity.

Operating in an atmosphere of constant tension and threat and without clear standards, oversight, or discipline, and without the ultimate sanction of criminal liability, abuses by private security contractors are inevitable.

Military Versus Contractors

The handling of allegations of excessive violence by these contractors stands in sharp contrast to the handling of similar cases involving the U.S. military. The military has clear authority to prosecute cases involving abuse by military personnel and in fact exercises this authority routinely. Though far from perfect, the military has established and devoted resources to build a comprehensive system of discipline and military justice by which soldiers, sailors, airmen, and Marines are subject to discipline or punished for their illegal actions. And while Human Rights First has been critical of DOD failures to hold senior officers accountable in cases involving abusive interrogation practices in Iraq and Afghanistan, we recognize that in general a regular and credible military criminal justice system in fact exists and is applied with some regularity to military personnel.

To date more than 60 U.S. military personnel have been court-martialed in the deaths of Iraqi citizens and more are under investigation. In contrast *not one* private contractor implicated in similar crimes in Iraq has been prosecuted. Human Rights First believes that the Justice Department's neglect has created a "shoot first, ask questions later—or *never*" attitude among some contractors. This endangers the local population amongst whom they operate. It also makes the job of the U.S. military harder by stoking animosities among the communities where military missions take place. This pattern of official disregard of contractor violence and abuse thus seriously undermines U.S. efforts to promote the rule of law in Iraq and Afghanistan and is in turn further endangering U.S. military personnel.

Responsibility Falls to the United States

The U.S. government has engaged the services of these private contractors and has made itself increasingly dependent on them. As a result, private contractors today perform many functions that even a decade ago would have been undertaken by the uniformed military. But when the United States or any nation deploys armed forces in conflicts abroad—even *private* armed forces—it has the responsibility to ensure that those forces comply with the law. Specifically, governments using private security forces in armed conflicts have the obligation to ensure that these forces are adequately vetted, trained, supervised, and held accountable. Individuals with histories of abusive or serious criminal conduct should not be put in a position to victimize others. They must be trained in the law of war and human rights, including how those laws are enforced through applicable domestic law. Private contractors also must be subject to effective oversight and supervision to ensure that such laws are observed. And finally, when abuses do occur, contractors must be investigated and held accountable under the law.

Human Rights First finds that:

- PSCs and other private contractors working for U.S. government agencies have committed and are committing serious crimes, with virtually no criminal accountability;

- Existing U.S. federal criminal law could be used in most cases to prosecute private contractors who use excessive violence, including contractors involved in abusive interrogations;

- The U.S. government has made no serious, systematic effort to investigate contractor abuse at Abu Ghraib; and

- Although some U.S. government officials assert there are major "holes" in the statutory framework, these assertions merely rationalize Justice Department inaction and executive branch indifference. Current federal law provides a substantial basis to try most private contractors involved in cases of abuse. Proposed legislation pending in Congress would clarify some ambiguities and enhance this authority.

Recommendations

In this report Human Rights First makes a number of practical recommendations for addressing and correcting this problem, which fall into three broad areas:

1. Action by Congress to strengthen federal criminal accountability mechanisms, and require more vigorous Justice Department investigation and prosecution of these cases.

2. Implementation by the Defense Department of its Uniform Code of Military Justice (UCMJ) jurisdiction as a limited and secondary mechanism for holding contractors criminally accountable in special circumstances.

3. Development by the executive branch of uniform contract practices and procedures and effective mechanisms for enhanced operational coordination and control of contractors.

Congress also should:

- Expand the list of serious felonies for which private contractors may be prosecuted under the Military Extraterritorial Jurisdiction Act (MEJA);

- Mandate comprehensive public executive branch reports to Congress on the employment and activities of PSCs, and on Justice and Defense Department efforts to hold PSCs accountable for crimes committed abroad, in order to enable Congress to perform effective oversight in this sphere; and

- Direct a thorough, comprehensive study of the roles of private contractors employed by the U.S. government in conflict settings, with a view specifically to identify whether there are areas of "core government" functions that should not be performed by private contractors. Based on our preliminary review, Human Rights First urges a presumption against private contractors' direct involvement in conducting interrogations.

The Accountability Gap Must Close

In June 2004, just weeks after revelations from Abu Ghraib had so embarrassed the [George W.] Bush administration, then–attorney general John Ashcroft announced the Passaro indictment—concerning a killing that occurred a full year earlier—in terms that suggested that thenceforth no private contractor implicated in serious law of war or human rights violations would ever again escape the long arm of the Justice Department:

> In the reports of abuse of detainees by United States personnel in Iraq and Afghanistan over the past two months, the world has witnessed a betrayal of America's most basic values by a small group of individuals. Their actions call us to the defense of our values—our belief in decency and respect for human life—through the enforcement of the law.

President Bush has made clear that the United States will not tolerate criminal acts of brutality such as those alleged in this indictment. The types of illegal abuse detailed run counter to our values and our policies and are not representative of our men and women in the military and associated personnel serving honorably and admirably for the cause of freedom.

Those who are responsible for such criminal acts will be investigated, prosecuted and, if found guilty, punished.

But in the three and a half years since Passaro's indictment, no other private contractors working in Iraq or Afghanistan have been indicted or prosecuted by the Justice Department for criminal violence or abuse toward local nationals.

The consequences of continued delay in closing this accountability gap are immense: Given the contractor population in Iraq, a simmering problem may boil into a crisis that could shape the eventual outcome of America's efforts in Iraq and reputation throughout the world. Perhaps it already has.

> "There really is no question that the majority of current Iraqi leaders want to work the American 'occupation' to as much of their economic and political advantage as possible."

Allegations Against Private Security Firms in Iraq Are Politicized

George H. Wittman

George H. Wittman is a member of the Committee on the Present Danger and was the founding chairman of the National Institute for Public Policy. In the following viewpoint, he maintains that allegations against American security contractors are a result of political opportunism by the Iraqi government, which wants to take more control of Iraqi security operations.

As you read, consider the following questions:

1. According to the author, what are the only two weapons available to American security contractors in Iraq?

2. How many people were killed in the Nisoor Square incident?

George H. Wittman, "The Wild West in Baghdad," *American Spectator*, September 27, 2007. Copyright © The American Spectator 2007. Reproduced by permission.

3. Why does the author believe that American security contractors are so vital?

It is interesting and not a little disturbing that the Iraqi Ministry of Interior, which long has been known as a tool of Shia militia operations, has chosen this moment to attempt to undercut U.S. security operations by launching an attack on the activities of American security contractors such as Blackwater USA.

What makes this matter worse is the complicity of Prime Minister [PM] Nouri al-Maliki, who immediately supported the Interior Ministry's claim of indiscriminate killing of Iraqi civilians by a Blackwater protection team guarding a State Department convoy in the Mansour district of Baghdad. Maliki, acting with a swiftness heretofore totally absent from his usual style of governance, rushed to condemn the American bodyguards and ordered the Blackwater firm decertified from operating in Iraq.

The Role of Security Contractors

American security contractors providing armed protection for Iraqi, American, and third country nationals have had only two weapons available to them: The first and most obvious are the automatic weapons they openly display, and second is the money they distribute as bribes to local police and militia forces to ensure area security through intelligence, firepower, and neighborhood tactical control.

The State Department motorcade of SUVs [sport-utility vehicles] was crossing Nisoor Square in western Baghdad when an explosion occurred, some small arms fire erupted, and the Blackwater guards immediately returned fire as the small convoy sped on. It's the sort of thing that has happened far too often. The Iraqi Interior Ministry investigated and announced eight people were killed outright, three more died in the hospital, twelve others were wounded. No American casualties were reported.

In the days following the PM's initial harsh reaction the prime minister's office denied that Maliki had ordered the de-certification and had not decided on the legal steps to be taken. An anonymous spokesman quoted by the Associated Press suggested financial compensation and an apology might suffice. The political damage had been done, though, and Blackwater, now referred to pejoratively as "mercenaries" by some American and European commentators, was placed on the political and public relations defensive.

Interesting Timing

In a suspicious coincidence of timing, Iraqi President Jalal Talabani called publicly for the release of an Iranian who had been captured by U.S. special ops forces in the Kurdish capital of Sulaimaniyah. The Iranian was charged with being a key member of the Iranian Revolutionary Guards' spec ops [special operations] unit known as Al Quds. Officially Talabani was upset because this Iranian operative was taken without first coordinating with the Kurdish provincial government.

It has been known for years that the Kurds have maintained covert contacts with Tehran [the Iranian capital], but having the president of Iraq, himself a Kurd, speak out demanding the release of an obviously important Iranian secret operative was more than surprising. One must question the timing of this action occurring in juxtaposition to PM Maliki's own attack on the leading American security firm in Iraq.

Political Backlash

Urged continuingly by the Americans to energize and reform their government, the Iraqi leadership has begun to push back. There is strong political pressure to curtail American influence on internal security affairs while at the same time not diminishing U.S. commitment to protect Iraq militarily and economically. The office of the president and prime minister, in separate security concerns, sent a signal not to be ignored.

HEADLESS HORSEMAN

IMMUNITY

BLACKWATER

JDCROWE PRESS-REGISTER
CROWETOONS.COM

© 2007 J. D. Crowe, Mobile Register and PoliticalCartoons.

Nonetheless, Blackwater and the other firms that supply civilian contractors providing personal and physical security in Iraq have been a necessary fact of life since after the initial invasion, and remain so. The fact is that this form of protection cannot be provided by coalition forces and certainly not the Iraqi government.

Selected Iraqi personnel have been an integral part of the protection teams where possible, but only after careful vetting. Here is the crux of the problem from the Iraqi government side. They want to control the choice of personnel of this special cadre of law enforcement as well as the political aspects of national security operations.

The arrogance of the private contractors, supposedly epitomized by Blackwater agents, from time to time has been a contributing factor. However, it must be realized that these former police and military experts augmented by ex-Special Forces and SEALs have had to face and overcome the heavily armed mafias of Iraqi sectarian, political and tribal organizations. This is not a job for Boy Scouts.

Political Opportunism

Iraqi politicians are well aware that the United States is in the midst of a national debate on our military presence in their country. There really is no question that the majority of current Iraqi leaders want to work the American "occupation" to as much of their economic and political advantage as possible. And they want to gain control of that advantage in whatever manner they can.

Taking over the lucrative private contracting of security operations is the first step in that plan.

> "*The* Maersk Alabama *hijacking . . . shows that the administration's legal and policy confusion over terrorism and piracy has contributed to the very problem at hand.*"

Somali Pirates Should Be Classified as War Criminals

John Yoo

John Yoo is a visiting fellow at the American Enterprise Institute for Public Policy Research; a professor of law at the University of California, Berkeley; and a former official in the U.S. Justice Department under George W. Bush. In the following viewpoint, he argues that unlike former presidents, Barack Obama treats the Somali pirates like common criminals and not war criminals or terrorists. This limits the military's options and adds to the problem of effectively addressing piracy.

As you read, consider the following questions:

1. How did President Theodore Roosevelt treat the Ion Perdicaris kidnapping by pirates in 1904?

2. How did President Thomas Jefferson treat Barbary pirates during his administration?

3. According to Yoo, what restrictions did President Barack Obama place on the Navy in dealing with Somali pirates?

"This government wants Perdicaris alive or Raisuli dead!"

That is how American presidents—in this case, the Teddy Roosevelt administration—used to respond to pirates.

In 1904, New Jersey native Ion Perdicaris was taken hostage by Moroccan bandits. They were led by Mulai Ahmed er Raisuli, who was known as the "Last of the Barbary Pirates."

Even though Perdicaris had moved from Trenton to Greece, Roosevelt believed that an attack on an American anywhere was an attack on Americans everywhere.

The president ordered seven battleships and a contingent of Marines to Morocco and issued the famous instructions demanding the return of Perdicaris. News of Roosevelt's tough stance ensured his renomination at the Republican convention that year.

Roosevelt was only continuing the attitude of past great presidents toward pirates. In 1801, Thomas Jefferson ended the payment of tribute to the Barbary pirates, who preyed on American shipping in the Mediterranean and enslaved U.S. sailors. He sent a naval squadron against the pirates with orders to "chastise their insolence" by "sinking, burning, or destroying their ships & vessels wherever you shall find them." That August, the USS *Enterprise* fought a three-hour duel with a pirate corsair, killing half its crew, cutting down its masts, throwing its guns overboard, and setting it adrift.

Contrast this with the recent hijacking of the *Maersk Alabama*. President Obama and, more particularly, the U.S. Navy, are to be praised for the eventual rescue of Capt. Richard Phillips and his American crew. The use of force against the

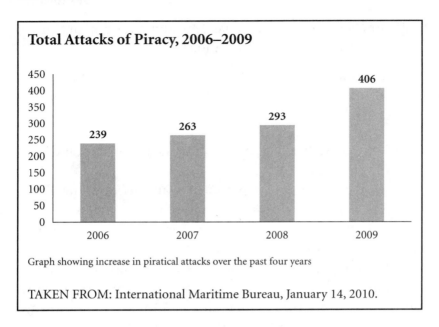

Total Attacks of Piracy, 2006–2009

Year	Attacks
2006	239
2007	263
2008	293
2009	406

Graph showing increase in piratical attacks over the past four years

TAKEN FROM: International Maritime Bureau, January 14, 2010.

pirates, carried out by the USS *Bainbridge* and Navy SEAL sharpshooters, displays the virtues of swift and decisive executive action.

The hijacking also shows that the administration's legal and policy confusion over terrorism and piracy has contributed to the very problem at hand. Roosevelt and Jefferson did not worry about whether Congress had authorized their actions against pirates, nor concern themselves with whether pirates deserved better treatment under international law. But the arguments of the Far Left, consumed by their hatred of Bush and his antiterrorism policies, has come back to haunt the Obama administration.

Under their theory of the war against al Qaeda, terrorism is really a crime, not an act of war. Terrorists are not illegal combatants (a category recognized by the Supreme Court in past wars and by other nations since Roman times to distinguish between proper soldiers of an enemy state and those who fight outside the laws of war). They do not fall under the Geneva Conventions, not because they choose to fight in violation of the rules of civilized warfare, but because they are just garden-variety criminals. Thus, these criminals cannot be arrested or searched without warrants, cannot be attacked with Predator drones, and must be tried in domestic courts.

The *Maersk Alabama* incident shows that these arguments have confused the White House's campaign against pirates. The Obama administration seems to think of pirates as criminals, who are to be arrested and hauled back to the United States for trial for the federal crime of piracy.

Obama's order that the Navy could fire only if Phillips were in imminent danger—which limited the sharpshooters to firing only after a pirate pointed an AK-47 at the captain's back—is basically the same rule that applies to police officers pursuing suspects. The FBI was on the scene conducting hostage negotiations.

Treat the pirates as they have consistently been since Roman times, as *hostis humani generis*, the enemy of all mankind, and the crisis would have been over faster. SEAL sharpshooters should have been able to fire whenever they had a clear shot, regardless of whether Phillips was threatened with imminent harm or death. The same would go for stopping pirate vessels. Rather than let pirates approach peaceful commercial shipping and only then seek to make arrests, our powerful Navy could simply hunt and destroy pirate ships and their land-based support networks "wherever" a commander "shall find them," in Jefferson's words.

But this would require the Obama administration to follow the Bush counterterrorism example by applying the rules of warfare to piracy. This does not mean that the United States cannot resort to its criminal laws, only that conflict with pirates can rise to the level of war and justify the use of military measures, too.

Pirates, of course, do not present as serious a threat to U.S. national security as al Qaeda or the Taliban (though there are concerns that some of the ransom money going to

Somali pirates may find its way to al Qaeda, which has had significant operations in Somalia). So far, piracy has primarily increased the costs of transporting oil and other goods through the crucial shipping routes of the Indian Ocean, and the dispatch of U.S. naval forces to the area seems to be suppressing the number of successful hijackings.

But the *Maersk Alabama* shows that piracy threatens a human cost as well, one that can be headed off only through the use of military force applied with a clear vision of piracy as an act of war, pirates as illegal combatants, and the United States as a sovereign nation with the right to clear the seas of this ages-old scourge.

> *"If the U.S. decides to pursue prosecution of the Somali 'pirate' in custody in a U.S. court, he would hopefully have a right to a defense."*

Somali Pirates Should Not Be Classified as War Criminals

Jeremy Scahill

Jeremy Scahill is a reporter, an author, and a fellow at the Nation Institute. In the following viewpoint, he maintains that President Barack Obama should ignore calls to try Somali pirates as enemy combatants or war criminals and instead try them in U.S. courts as criminals subject to U.S. criminal laws and procedure.

As you read, consider the following questions:

1. What does Scahill view as the three key questions about using military force on the Somali pirates?

2. According to legal scholar Scott Horton, what is an interesting distinction between the Obama and Bush administrations' positions on pirates?

3. How does Scahill describe a possible Somali pirate defense scenario?

Jeremy Scahill, "Will Obama Prosecute the Captured Somali 'Pirate' in a U.S. Court?" Alternet.org, April 13, 2009. Reproduced by permission.

The airwaves, newspapers and Web sites have been saturated with coverage of the rescue of Captain Richard Phillips, the U.S. citizen who was being held by four Somali "pirates" on a small lifeboat in the Indian Ocean, following the unsuccessful attempt by the Somalis to take control of the U.S.-flagged vessel, the *Maersk Alabama*, a ship owned by a Pentagon contractor.

Using Legal Force

While details are still emerging, there are definitely some serious questions looming about how the decision to use lethal military force was put into play—in particular three key questions:

1. The legality of the killing of the three Somali men;

2. The political decision to kill them in light of long-term potential consequences;

3. The legal status of the fourth Somali "pirate" allegedly in U.S. custody.

First the background: We are told that on Friday, President [Barack] Obama gave the military the green light to use lethal force to rescue Phillips. We also know that a group of "Somali elders" believed they were negotiating with the U.S. to try to bring about a peaceful resolution to the crisis. Reports indicate that the Somali elders asked that the four Somalis be allowed to return freely to Somalia without being prosecuted in exchange for releasing Phillips. That was reportedly rejected by the U.S. On Sunday, the Somalis were told the negotiations were over and that the Americans "had another action." Shortly after that, lethal force was used—with Navy SEAL snipers on board the USS *Bainbridge* shooting dead three of the Somali men. The Navy says the snipers took the action because they believed Phillips's life was in "imminent danger"— this allegedly came when a Somali was pointing an AK-47 at Phillips's back. A fourth Somali citizen is in custody, though it is unclear when exactly he was taken by the U.S. Reports indicate that he had been stabbed in the hand in the initial "pirate" raid on the *Maersk Alabama* and, before the Sunday raid, had voluntarily left the lifeboat holding Phillips to seek medical attention from the U.S. warships and/or to negotiate with the U.S. side.

Legal Issues

I have been in touch with two well-respected legal scholars, Francis Boyle from the University of Illinois College of Law and Scott Horton, a military and constitutional law expert. Both agree that the U.S. had *legal* justification to use lethal force against the "pirates." Boyle said, "Technically, piracy is a felony under U.S. law. And deadly force can be used against someone involved in the commission of an ongoing felony."

For his part, Horton said: "The legal rule historically is that pirates on the high seas are fair game for any country's military. In this case they kidnapped a captain and threatened to kill him, so the use of lethal force against them was fine from a legal perspective. (The bigger question was whether it was a wise thing to do, of course, but that requires an assessment of the entire tactical situation, about which I don't know enough)."

On that question, Vice Admiral Bill Gortney, head of the U.S. Navy's Bahrain-based Fifth Fleet, seemed to realize that there may be significant consequences for the decision to kill the Somali men. "This could escalate violence in this part of the world, no question about it," Gortney said. As Reuters reported, "Somali pirates have generally not harmed their hostages and officials fear they could now act more violently."

As one "pirate" said, "The French and the Americans will regret starting this killing. We do not kill, but take only ransom. We shall do something to anyone we see as French or American from now." Another added, "As long as there is no

Don't Believe the Hype

Modern pirates bear little resemblance to popular ro-
mantic Hollywood characters. Increasingly violent and
greedy, their actions seem an affront to the very ideals of
Western civilization. Armchair admirals and politicians
are quick to shake their fists, avowing, "Something must
be done." Maritime industry is quick to follow, with un-
settling incident accounts and dire financial projections.
Yet, more informed analysis of piracy reveals that the impact in blood and treasure is altogether minimal.

Indeed, common misperceptions abound. While
maritime piracy incidents capture media attention and
generate international calls for action, the piracy threat is
in fact overstated. It is nothing more than high-seas
criminal activity, better addressed by law enforcement
agencies than warships. As a localized nuisance, it should
not serve to shape maritime force structure or strategy.

John Patch, "The Overstated Threat,"
Proceedings, vol. 134, December 2008.

just government in Somalia, we will still be the coast guard. . . .
If we get an American, we will take revenge."

Prosecuting the Pirates

On the issue of jurisdiction to prosecute the fourth Somali
"pirate," Horton said, "Pirates can be tried anywhere that exercises jurisdiction. Here they attacked a U.S.-flag vessel, which
means that the United States would have criminal law jurisdiction if it chose to exercise it."

There are certain to be calls from blood-thirsty lunatics to
send this Somali man to Guantánamo or Bagram [detention
centers] with right-wingers like Newt Gingrich and Cal Tho-

mas wrapping this into their tired "Obama is weak on terror" narrative. As Thomas wrote last week on the Fox News Web site:

> What will the Obama administration do if the pirates are captured alive? He won't send them to Gitmo [Guantánamo Bay detention camp], which he is closing down. Will they get ACLU [American Civil Liberties Union] lawyers? Will there be testimony from a "pirates rights" group? Will they be released on a technicality after a trial in U.S. courts? If there is not as forceful a response as there was during the [Thomas] Jefferson administration, it will invite more of these incidents. The world's tyrants are watching to see how President Obama reacts. The message they get will determine how they respond to America and whether we will be in greater peril.

Indeed, the *Wall Street Journal* on Sunday called for the Somali man in custody to be "transferred to Guantánamo and held as an 'enemy combatant,' or whatever the Obama administration prefers to call terrorists." On this point, Horton points out an interesting distinction between the Obama and Bush administrations' positions on "pirates," particularly as it relates to the "terrorist" label.

> The big legal issue is surrounding calling them "terrorists," which the Bushies did with regularity and Obama resisted. I think that Obama and his people are correct. These people were motivated by the desire to make money, pure and simple, which makes them conventional pirates. If they were labeled "terrorists," the insurance company and the ship charter company wouldn't be able to negotiate with them or make a payment. Pirates they can still pay off, which will often be the most sensible and least costly solution.

Following the Rule of Law

If the U.S. decides to pursue prosecution of the Somali "pirate" in custody in a U.S. court, he would hopefully have a right to a defense (which would clearly enrage the crazies) and the nature of that defense could well depend on what type of legal counsel he ends up with and how his lawyers present the motives of his actions, as described to them, in attempting to seize the *Maersk Alabama*. This could be a major test of Obama's legal interpretation of the rights of prisoners taken by the U.S. in unusual circumstances (to put it mildly). In an era when due process has been trashed in the U.S. and prisoners have been tortured at CIA [Central Intelligence Agency] "black sites" and held without trial for years at Guantánamo and elsewhere, Obama should allow exactly what Thomas and his ilk fear so much—respect for the legal rights of prisoners held by the U.S.

So what would a "pirate" defense actually look like? Remember, some Somalis—and other international observers—do not exactly see the "pirates" as being 100% unjustified in their actions. This form of "piracy" really escalated after the 1991 collapse of the Somali government and Western ships allegedly dumping waste off the Somali coast and devastating the Somali fishing industry, a primary source of income in the Somali coastal areas where many of the "pirates" are based.

Avoiding the Controversy

If Obama elects not to take the terrible option of sending the man to Guantánamo, it will be interesting to see if Obama elects to bring him to the U.S. or, as has been suggested by some, prosecute him in Kenya.

As Professor Boyle pointed out, "Certainly if he were tried in a United States federal district court, he could try to make the points [about dumping, etc.], which is why they might send him to Kenya to avoid all of that. . . . If I remember correctly, under the Geneva Convention definition of piracy (which is not precisely the same thing as the federal statute), the crime of piracy must be for a private purpose, not a public purpose. So he might be able to raise these issues on the question of intent—that he acted for a public purpose, not a private purpose."

Boyle later e-mailed me the following quote from St. Augustine:

> Kingdoms without justice are similar to robber barons. And so if justice is left out, what are kingdoms except great robber bands? For what are robber bands except little kingdoms? The band also is a group of men governed by the orders of a leader, bound by a social compact, and its booty is divided according to a law agreed upon. If by repeatedly adding desperate men this plague grows to the point where it holds territory and establishes a fixed seat, seizes cities and subdues peoples, then it more conspicuously assumes the name of kingdom, and this name is now openly granted to it, not for any subtraction of cupidity, but by addition of impunity. For it was an elegant and true reply that was made to Alexander the Great by a certain pirate whom he had captured. When the king asked him what he was thinking of, that he should molest the sea, he said with defiant independence: "The same as you when you molest the world! Since I do this with a little ship I am called a pirate. You do it with a great fleet and are called an emperor."

> "The ICC's office of the prosecutor has made strides in investigating and indicting crimes of sexual violence in other countries, largely thanks to continued pressure from local and international women's NGOs."

Groups That Use Mass Rape Should Be Tried as War Criminals

Alyson Zureick

Alyson Zureick is a writer based in New York. In the following viewpoint, she notes that for the first time in history, the International Criminal Court (ICC) decided to pursue a prosecution of crimes of mass rape, calling it a "a significant step forward for African civil society groups and their international partners."

As you read, consider the following questions:

1. On what country does the ICC's new investigation of mass rape allegations focus?

2. How many rapes have been documented so far in this investigation?

3. How many incidents of rape have been verified by the prosecutor?

On May 22nd, Luis Moreno-Ocampo, the chief prosecutor for the International Criminal Court (ICC), made a landmark announcement: For the first time in its short history, the Court was opening an investigation that, from the start, would prioritize crimes of mass rape along with mass killings.

A Step Forward

The prosecutor's announcement was a significant step forward for African civil society groups and their international partners across the continent that have been working to collect evidence and push the ICC to investigate and prosecute crimes of sexual violence. Yet this victory has been hard won, and there is no guarantee that the ICC's new-found focus on sexual violence will translate into long-term gains for victims of these crimes.

The ICC's newest investigation will examine alleged war crimes and crimes against humanity committed in the Central African Republic (CAR) between late 2002 and early 2003, following a failed coup attempt by General François Bozizé against the civilian president, Ange-Félix Patassé, and just prior to a second, successful coup attempt by Bozizé. (He is now the president of CAR). Human rights groups and the Bozizé government claim that Patassé's troops terrorized the civilian population around the capital, Bangui, to punish them for supporting the first attempted coup. These groups also claim that the troops were assisted by militias from the neighboring Democratic Republic of the Congo (DRC) loyal to Congolese official Jean-Pierre Bemba. Moreno-Ocampo has insisted that his office is not yet targeting any particular suspects. The investigations are expected to last about 18 months.

A Welcome First

The situation in CAR is the first conflict the ICC has investigated in which mass rapes appear to have outnumbered mass killings. Local and international NGOs have documented more than 1,000 incidents of rape during the time period in question, and the ICC's office of the prosecutor has verified 600 incidents. "Many groups of women have taken immense risks to bring forward their testimony," said Béatrice Le Fraper Du Hellen, director of the Jurisdiction, Complementarity and Cooperation Division of the ICC. "Some are very threatened, and we have taken protective measures for many of them prior to announcing the investigation."

Much of the testimony on sexual violence submitted to the ICC was gathered by local NGOs, like the Organization for Compassion and the Development of Families in Distress (OCODEFAD). "We found in 2002 that survivors of the violence had come together to take care of the victims of sexual violence because they were stigmatized in their communities," reports Marceau Sivieude, the Africa Desk Director for the prominent human rights organization Federation for Human Rights (FIDH). "They had also decided to gather evidence of these crimes and fight for national justice."

Between 2002 and 2007, FIDH assisted OCODEFAD and the Central African Human Rights League (LCDH) in gathering testimony and lobbying the ICC to investigate. FIDH submitted its first report to the office of the prosecutor in early 2003, but received no response. The ICC did not begin an official analysis of the situation until months after the CAR government referred it to the Court in 2004. As the ICC began its analysis, reports and testimony continued to flow in from local groups. By the time the ICC was ready to launch an official investigation, it was obvious that investigating sexual violence needed to be a priority.

Correcting Its Course

The ICC prosecutor's focus on sexual violence in CAR has been so widely hailed in part because, like its cousins, the international tribunals for the former Yugoslavia and Rwanda, the ICC has had a spotty record of addressing crimes of sexual violence. Most notoriously, the office of the prosecutor failed to bring charges of sexual crimes in its first case, that of Thomas Lubanga Dyilo. Ample documentation by international organizations and local NGOs indicated that the armed militia group Lubanga led had committed widespread abuses in the DRC.

"The evidence was clear that rape and other forms of sexual violence had been widespread and systematic," said Brigid Inder, the executive director of the Women's Initiatives for Gender Justice, the only international women's NGO working on sexual violence with local women's groups in each of the countries currently on the ICC's docket. "The prosecutor's first investigations in the DRC were narrow and poorly conducted. They failed to pursue and follow up on leads in relation to gender-based crimes." Consequently, when the time came for the ICC to issue an arrest warrant for Lubanga, it only had sufficient evidence for charges of child soldier conscription—a serious charge but one that hardly reflects the range of crimes documented in eastern DRC.

Today, Congolese NGOs are, like their CAR counterparts, working to make sure these problems do not recur. They have ramped up their efforts to document sexual violence in eastern DRC and gather evidence that will assist the ICC in bringing such charges in future indictments, according to Christian Hemedi, president of the Coalition of Congolese NGOs for the ICC in Kinshasa. The Coalition coordinates efforts by NGOs in the DRC to provide information and evidence to the ICC and encourage the DRC government to cooperate with the ICC. The Women's Initiatives for Gender Justice is also

Mass Rape as Genocide

Sudan's president, Omar Hassan Ahmad al-Bashir, stands accused of—among other horrible crimes—masterminding the use of rape as a form of genocide against several ethnic groups in Darfur. In the coming weeks, three judges of the International Criminal Court in The Hague [city in The Netherlands] will decide whether that controversial charge will be included in the likely arrest warrant against him.

David Scheffer,
"When Mass Rape Turns into Genocide,"
Los Angeles Times, *November 13, 2008.*

continuing its work with local women's NGOs to document sexual violence and lobby the ICC on these issues.

Going Forward on Mass Rape Prosecutions

Civil society efforts appear to have had an effect on the ICC. A second investigation is under way in the DRC, and the ICC anticipates that a third will be launched in the near future. It is expected that sexual violence will be covered in the resulting indictments, Le Fraper Du Hellen said. The ICC's office of the prosecutor has made strides in investigating and indicting crimes of sexual violence in other countries, largely thanks to continued pressure from local and international women's NGOs. In the case of Darfur, the prosecutor's office at first hesitated to pursue charges of rape, fearing that it would take too long to investigate and that the acts would be too difficult to prove, Inder said. The office quickly changed its mind after further information on gender-based crimes was provided, and in early May, the ICC issued arrest warrants for two

Sudanese leaders on counts of crimes against humanity and war crimes. Rape is included in the charges for both men.

Despite some advances, significant gaps remain. The ICC has issued five arrest warrants for leaders of the rebel group the Lord's Resistance Army (LRA) in Uganda, but only two have been charged with rape despite existing evidence that indicates each of the suspects could be reasonably charged with this crime, Inder said. And the ICC office of the prosecutor continues to lack a gender advisor who would be a part of the senior decision-making team. "The position has been advertised in the past but never filled," said Inder. The ICC does run a Gender and Children Unit that undertakes psychosocial assessment of witnesses and victims of gender-based crimes, though the unit lacks the specific legal mandate that a gender advisor would possess.

Additionally, the ICC faces procedural challenges for securing justice for those who suffered during conflict. In the case of CAR, there is concern that, given the four-year gap between the end of the conflict in question and the beginning of the ICC's investigations, it will be difficult for the prosecutor to find evidence that will stand up in court, Sivieude said. The ICC is a court of last resort, and could not begin its work in CAR until the national court determined that the domestic legal system was not capable of handling the proceedings.

A Difficult Case to Prove

Experience with the international criminal tribunals for the former Yugoslavia and Rwanda have also shown that it can be difficult to convince judges that military and civilian leaders are accountable for crimes of sexual violence committed under their leadership when they themselves are not physically present, according to Kelly Askin, a senior legal officer with the Open Society Justice Initiative. In CAR, it will be important for the prosecutor to present solid evidence that key leaders commissioned, committed or had command responsibility for acts of sexual violence.

Thus, while the ICC's newly announced investigations are a step in the right direction, the Court has its work cut out for it when it comes to actually collecting criminal evidence and prosecuting these crimes in CAR and other countries. Given the Court's uneven record on these issues, local and international activists are prepared to continue lobbying hard for these crimes to be taken seriously in the Court's proceedings.

"The gains that have been made for victims of sexual violence have been hard fought by a small number of local and international women's NGOs every step of the way," Inder said. "Continued pressure will be needed to ensure that the ICC follows through on this progress and ends impunity for perpetrators of such crimes."

| "Sexual violence remains the invisible war crime."

Rape Is Not Vigorously Prosecuted as a War Crime

Binaifer Nowrojee

Binaifer Nowrojee is an author, the Human Rights Program clinical instructor at Harvard Law School, and the director of the Open Society Initiative for East Africa. In the following viewpoint, she applauds recent efforts to investigate and prosecute incidents of mass rape, but contends that these efforts have to be vigorous and consistent. Nowrojee notes that violence against women is usually ignored by international justice institutions.

As you read, consider the following questions:

1. According to the author, what are some of the things that have hindered attempts to bring mass rapists to justice in the past?

2. How does the author characterize mass rape investigations in general?

Binaifer Nowrojee, "We Can Do Better Investigating and Prosecuting International Crimes of Sexual Violence," Paper presented at the Colloquium of Prosecutors of International Criminal Tribunals, Arusha, Tanzania, WomensRightsCoalition.org, November 24–25, 2004. Reproduced by permission of the author.

3. How is sexual violence dismissed, according to the author?

"African women will not talk about rape."

"We haven't received any real complaints [about rape]."

"We don't have the evidence."

"Criminal prosecutors are here to get convictions, not make political statements."

"We don't have the evidence."

"Women's rights activists are trying to make the issue of rape more important than it should be."

"Of course we are committed to prosecuting rape, but you're barking up the wrong tree with this guy [Akayesu]."

"The rapes were a case of libido, not genocide crimes."

"We don't have the evidence."

"We need to cut the unnecessary charges, like rape."

"They [the accused] are going to be convicted of genocide anyway, so why do we need to bring rape charges?"

These are a few of the statements that I have heard over the years from international investigators and prosecutors about why the rape charges should not be pursued in their cases.

As any good international prosecutor knows, sexual violence against women and girls in situations of armed conflict constitutes a clear breach of international law. Perpetrators of sexual violence can be convicted for rape as a war crime, a crime against humanity, or as an act of genocide or torture, if their actions meet the elements of each. Leaders in positions of command responsibility who knew or should have had reason to know of such abuses and who took no steps to stop subordinates who committed sex crimes can, and should, be held accountable.

Rape as a Weapon of War

In the course of the armed conflict in eastern Democratic Republic of the Congo (DRC), tens of thousands of women and girls have been victims of systematic rape and sexual assault committed by combatant forces. Women and girls have been attacked in their homes, in the fields or as they go about their daily activities. Many have been raped more than once or have suffered gang rapes. In many cases, women and young girls have been taken as sex slaves by combatants. Rape of men and boys has also taken place. Rape has often been preceded or followed by the deliberate wounding, torture (including torture of sexual nature) or killing of the victim. Rapes have been committed in public and in front of family members, including children. Some women have been raped next to the corpses of family members.

Amnesty International USA,
"Democratic Republic of Congo:
Mass Rape—Time for Remedies," 2009.
www.amnestyusa.org.

Crimes Must Be Investigated and Prosecuted

It is therefore part of the mandate of justice institutions prosecuting international crimes to address sexual violence. It is the job of every international prosecutor to effectively investigate and prosecute this crime with the same seriousness as other international crimes under his or her brief. International courts are examining the most egregious atrocities committed in the course of some of the world's worst conflicts. Without exception in these places, combatants have terrorized women and girls with rape and other forms of sexual violence.

Thousands of women and girls are routinely subjected to brutal rapes, sexual assaults, sexual slavery, and mutilation during conflict. Rape and other forms of sexual violence are regularly used as weapons of war, instruments of terror, serving to further military and political goals of the conflict. Rape of women in wartime is a deliberate act of dominance and violence that targets women's sexuality and gender roles.

Given its routine widespread and systematic use, virtually every case coming before the international criminal courts should seek accountability for sexual violence crimes. Yet, this is in fact not the case. Sexual violence remains the invisible war crime. It remains a continuing challenge in the fight against invisibility to ensure that women's experiences are not ignored in this era of international justice.

Efforts to Prosecute Must Be Consistent

Much has been written by legal scholars celebrating the international tribunals and the International Criminal Court as an important step forward in ending impunity for sexual violence against women. It must be acknowledged that there have been some commendable efforts made at various periods by international investigators and prosecutors, but the problem is that they have not been consistently pursued nor institutionalized. And while it is true that there have been some gains made in that these institutions formally recognize that sexual violence is a crime, and even nominally include such charges, their efforts have still been fraught with problems that have prevented them from comprehensively and sensitively rendering justice to women victims. Despite the rhetoric and the repeated pronouncements by international prosecutors expressing a commitment to prosecuting rape, here is the unfortunate record: Squandered opportunities, periods of neglect, and repeated mistakes have caused setbacks to effective investigations and prosecutions of sexual violence crimes by international courts.

Sexual violence charges are not always brought by international prosecutors, sometimes even when a prosecuting attorney is in possession of evidence. If brought, these charges are often added belatedly, as an afterthought, in amendments that are not properly integrated into cases. At the outset, prosecutors do not craft and follow a consistently defined strategy of how this crime fit into the policies of the accused war criminals, accordingly, different trial teams adopt different approaches. As a result, no single identified work plan is pursued consistently by all investigators and trial lawyers that integrates sexual violence charges appropriately into all the cases. Investigators are not always trained in dealing with this issue and do not pay sufficient attention to consistently employing effective investigative techniques to fully document the crimes against women. This results in a situation where shoddy investigative work later results in rape charges being withdrawn by trial attorneys that are not interested or able to rectify the investigative shortfalls. As pressure mounts on prosecuting teams at the ad hoc tribunals to speed up trials and to cut unnecessary charges, sexual violence charges are sometimes seen to be in that category. How, and whether, rape charges get included in a case often is based on the individual commitment of an investigator or trial attorney rather than an institutional policy.

Reversing the Legacy

Historically, there has been a silence surrounding the sex crimes against women that downplays their suffering and renders them invisible. Sexual violence is often dismissed as the private act of a combatant or an unfortunate by-product of war. In a post-conflict situation, this silence usually continues, exacerbated by the stigma attached to rape. Although rape and other forms of sexual violence often constitute torture, genocide, mutilation and enslavement, they have, with rare exception, not been punished with the same seriousness as other war crimes. That continues to remain the case.

Reversing this legacy remains the obligation of every transitional justice institution charged with prosecuting crimes committed during conflict.

Periodical Bibliography

The following articles have been selected to supplement the diverse views presented in this chapter.

Brian Bennett	"America's Other Army," *Time*, October 18, 2007.
Christopher Caldwell	"No Surrender to Somali Pirate Thugs," *Time*, April 27, 2009.
Imani Cheers	"A Weapon of War," *Newsweek*, June 25, 2008.
Brett Joshpe	"Pirates' Rights," *American Spectator*, November 24, 2008.
Fred Kaplan	"How to Beat the Pirates," *Slate*, April 15, 2009. www.slate.com.
Ed Morales	"The Role of Private Defense Contractors Needs to Be Curbed," *Progressive*, September 12, 2009.
Rod Nordland	"The Evil Solution," *Newsweek*, December 18, 2008.
Chuck Norris	"Jefferson, U.S. Hostages and Somali Pirates," WorldNetDaily, April 20, 2009. www.wnd.com.
Veronique de Rugy	"Paying the Pirate's Price," *Reason*, July 2009.
Jacob Sullum	"Lawless Justice," *Reason*, December 10, 2008.
George H. Wittman	"The Somali-Kenya Connection," *American Spectator*, November 6, 2009.
Adam Zagorin	"Blackwater's Florida Court Woes," *Time*, November 7, 2007.

How Should the United States Address War Crimes?

Chapter Preface

What is the responsibility of states to intervene in the face of mass genocide and crimes of humanity perpetrated by a government against its people? How can an oppressed and victimized group find help if its government is the one oppressing and victimizing it? And what responsibility does the international community have to intervene? These questions haunted the international community after the devastating failure to prevent horrible atrocities in Kosovo, East Timor, and Darfur. With reports of widespread mass rape, genocide, and crimes against humanity virtually unabated, observers realized that a strong need existed to emphasize the security of the community and individual—and not only the state—in the international security community. This led to the establishment of the Responsibility to Protect (R2P) doctrine.

In December 2001 the International Commission on Intervention and State Sovereignty (ICISS) released a report exploring the key issue on international intervention: when the right of a state to control its own sovereignty must yield to international efforts to protect against the most egregious violations of humanitarian and international law. A high-level panel was formed in 2003 to study the question, which focused on how the United Nations (UN) should address the most serious security threats facing the world in the new century. In December 2004 the panel released its report, titled *A More Secure World: Our Shared Responsibility*. It was within this report that the principle of R2P was first endorsed.

It didn't take long for many nations to embrace the idea of R2P. Support for a formal commitment to the ideals presented in the report began to grow. In September 2005 a World Summit was held that gave many nations an opportunity to put their commitment in writing. The World Summit Outcome Document states that heads of state and government agree that "each individual state has the primary responsibility to protect its populations from genocide, war crimes, crimes against humanity and ethnic cleansing." Moreover, that "when a state manifestly fails in its protection responsibilities, and peaceful means are inadequate, the international community must take stronger measures, including the collective use of force."

The United States, however, did not rush to embrace the R2P doctrine. Conceding that some dire situations require international intervention, critics in the United States argued that it is easy to call for military intervention when other nations would be primarily responsible for doing the work. In addition, it would be difficult to ask American soldiers to intervene in every humanitarian crisis around the world at any given time. Some critics doubt the efficacy of an international effort when other UN-directed efforts have turned out to be failures.

Advocates assert that U.S. acceptance and implementation of the R2P doctrine will restore American leadership in the world and reestablish U.S. credibility in the international security arena. They argue that it is within U.S. interests to prevent mass atrocities, enforce international law, and foster international peace.

How the United States should engage the R2P doctrine is one of the issues examined in this chapter. Other viewpoints debate whether war criminals should be incarcerated in U.S. jails and whether terrorists should be tried in civilian courts or military tribunals.

> "The United States must lead in the es-
> tablishment of effective, legitimate and
> consistently applied mechanisms—
> based on the rule of law—to prevent
> and react to mass atrocities, as well as
> guide the rebuilding of societies shat-
> tered by such atrocities."

The United States Should Embrace the Responsibility to Protect Doctrine

Richard H. Cooper and Juliette Voinov Kohler

Richard H. Cooper is the convenor and Juliette Voinov Kohler is the deputy-convenor of the R2P Coalition, an organization that works to convince the American people and their government leaders to embrace the Responsibility to Protect (R2P) doctrine and join the International Criminal Court (ICC). In the follow-ing viewpoint, Cooper and Kohler argue that it is time for the United States to make the R2P doctrine a flagship of its foreign policy to help abolish mass atrocities.

Richard H. Cooper and Juliette Voinov Kohler, "The 'Responsibility to Protect' and the United States of America," *The 'Responsibility to Protect': The New Global Moral Compact*, 2006. Copyright © August 2006 Richard H. Cooper and Juliette Voinov Kohler. Reproduced by permission Palgrave MacMillan Ltd.

As you read, consider the following questions:

1. According to the authors, what is the overarching goal of the Responsibility to Protect doctrine?

2. Why has the perception of the United States dropped so precipitously in recent years, according to the report?

3. What are three reasons why the United States should act upon the Responsibility to Protect doctrine?

The United States Current Foreign Policy and the "Responsibility of Protect"

a) From a minimum common denominator. . .

The endorsement of the doctrine of the "responsibility to protect" during the General Assembly 2005 World Summit means that the international community was able to find a common base upon which to elaborate further measures aimed at preventing and reacting to atrocity crimes as well as rebuilding societies shattered by genocide, war crimes, crimes against humanity and ethnic cleansing.

The overarching goal of the "responsibility to protect" is to free humanity from the commission of atrocity crimes. This revolutionary doctrine offers the perspective of a holistic approach that transcends time lines—prevention, reaction, rebuilding—and calls for the use of a variety of tools—diplomatic, legal, judicial, economic, social, police and military.

The unanimous embrace of the "responsibility to protect" is but one step, even if historical, towards actually dealing with mass atrocities: it is the minimum common denominator states with various and sometimes opposing national interests could agree upon. The next step—the strengthening and the implementation of all the components of the doctrine of the "responsibility to protect"—is still a long and tortuous way ahead.

A first step towards the implementation of some aspects of the "responsibility to protect" was taken on 28 April 2006 when the Security Council adopted its resolution on the protection of civilians in armed conflict. It is the first time that the Security Council endorses the doctrine of the "responsibility to protect," a step that has a major significance since it is the UN body that has primary responsibility for dealing with threats to international peace and security, including atrocity crimes. Although the scope of the resolution is not the same as that of the doctrine of the responsibility to protect, the Security Council requires specific steps to be taken by states and the international community in order to protect civilians. These include:

- To end impunity and prosecute those responsible for atrocity crimes;

- To ensure that the mandates of peacekeeping, political and peace-building missions include *where appropriate and on a case-by-case basis*, provisions regarding the protection of civilians and clear guidelines on what missions can do to achieve this goal.

b) . . . to a fully fledged answer to atrocity crimes

During the negotiations of the World Summit Outcome, our government expressed support for the "responsibility to protect," underlining that there is "clear" risk to international peace and security in cases of genocide, war crimes, crimes against humanity and ethnic cleansing. Our government underscored that the international community must, in these circumstances, be prepared to use peaceful means to protect populations. Our government, however, opposed any step aimed at regulating the use of force to protect populations from mass atrocities. As Gareth Evans wrote: the US "very definitively did not want any guidelines adopted that could limit in any way the Security Council's—and by extension its own—complete freedom to make judgments on a case-by-case basis."

Today, the slaughter in Darfur is in the public eye. We owe it in part to a handful of dedicated journalists and to an amazing grassroots movement who is appealing to our country to act. Even our officials invoke the norm of the "responsibility to protect" to call for stronger measures in order to both induce the Sudanese government to comply with its "responsibility to protect" as well as to deliver protection to the victims of mass atrocities. Yet we must go beyond. Mass atrocities do not deserve *ad hoc* responses. *Ad hoc* responses are inefficient and costly, not only in terms of financial costs. *Ad hoc* responses have great political costs. And they waste precious time. *Ad hoc* responses have no logic but to lead to institutionalized and standing mechanisms. We cannot, should not, have to nearly reinvent the rule each time our conscience is so shocked that we feel the urge to march down the streets of Washington or Chicago.

More than fifty years have elapsed since the founders of the United Nations laid down their vision of a peaceful world. Their vision encompassed a collective system of security which was only credible and effective because the promise of peace could be delivered, if required, on the ground. Yes indeed, it is time to build on the norm of the "responsibility to protect" and to fulfill the promises of the founding fathers of the United Nations.

These are exciting and decisive times for humankind. It is our aspiration that we, the American people, take advantage of such remarkable times to lead the way for the abolition of mass atrocities. It is our wish that the American people and its leaders will seize this opportunity and make the "responsibility to protect" a flagship of our country's foreign policy. It is our hope that a contemporary historian will, in the future, be remembered for saying:

> "The way America has strengthened and implemented the 'responsibility to protect' has done more for us and the world than all our former victories and all our diplomacy."

An Opportunity to Reassert America's leadership

Strengthening and implementing the doctrine of the "responsibility to protect" can help the United States restore its credibility in the international arena. And this, to our chagrin, we badly need.

a) The perception of the United States in the world

During the 1990s, the United States had a commanding position in the world. Today, the perception of our country has dramatically changed. A majority of people in the world feels that our country is not having a positive influence in the world. According to a 2005 study by the Pew Research Center, "anti-Americanism is deeper and broader now than at any time in modern history." Why? The size and overwhelming power of the United States is one part of the answer. The rest of the world fears and resents this colossus. Even in the United Kingdom, the United States' most trusted ally, 55% see our country as a threat to global peace. This fear is exacerbated, and that's the other part of the answer, by the way the United States behaves at the international level: too quick to act unilaterally, not properly addressing the world's problems (such as climate change, peace in the Middle East, or the International Criminal Court) and widening the gulf between the rich and the poor.

Let's face it. The anti-American sentiment stems from a widespread disagreement over specific policy issues coupled with the unfortunate perception that our government is acting in an arrogant way and on the basis of double standards. How far have we come from the Wilsonian dream whereby the world will turn to America for those moral inspirations that lie at the basis of all freedom, the dream that America puts human rights above all other rights, and that her flag is the flag not only of America but of humanity?

It's time for America to get right.

b) Why the United States should act upon the responsibility to protect

Implementing the "responsibility to protect" has a broad range of fundamentally important practical implications:

- To prevent or, to the very least, put an end to mass atrocities;

- To hold perpetrators of mass atrocities accountable for their acts, thereby putting an end to impunity in cases of genocide, crimes against humanity and war crimes;

- To promote reconciliation in crisis-afflicted societies;

- To contribute to the building of stable societies less prone to mass atrocities;

- To reinforce the rule of law by ensuring the effectiveness of—and compliance with—international law, in particular the UN and the ICC;

- To guarantee and enforce international justice;

- To contribute to the maintenance of international peace and security.

All these objectives are in the interest of America for they lead to a more just and stable world community. For some of us, these goals are sufficiently noble and wise to justify a passionate engagement in favor of embracing and fully realizing the potential of the norm of the "responsibility to protect." Yet for others, these practical implications might seem too abstract. How palatable is the "maintenance of international peace and security?" How much does the delivery of justice to a victim of mass atrocities in a distant country directly impact me, as an individual? You may ask yourself: why should I care beyond feeling sorry for those miserable people? Or, is it that we find refuge in the dehumanization of a situation? Do we allow ourselves to consider that the victims of mass atrocities are no more than the "miserable creatures" that our ancestors saw in the victims of slavery?

Beyond the political and legal arguments, there are two distinct and compelling cases to be made in favor of the "responsibility to protect." The fast one stems from prudence and enlightened self-interest. The second is commanded by ethics.

Prudence and Enlightened Self-Interest

Preventing and putting an end to atrocity crimes is in every individual's own interest. Nobody would want to be the victim of genocide, of torture, of slavery. Everyone wants to live in a society where the chance of occurrence of mass atrocities is null. Every society should be built in a way that will prevent the commission of genocide, crimes against humanity as well as war crimes. This is why the sum of individuals that compose American society certainly want to live in a country whose leadership has embraced and fully implements the "responsibility to protect" on its very soil. This means, for example, promoting tolerance between communities, fighting social and economic exclusion, promoting justice and the rule of law, ensuring our leadership's accountability, and making sure our military troops are properly trained about the *jus in bello* i.e. the laws applicable in warfare.

Embracing the international community's "responsibility to protect" populations in other countries from genocide, crimes against humanity and war crimes is also in each individual's self-interest. We will agree with many that it seems more difficult to make the case for the global dimension of the "responsibility to protect." But we only agree in as far as this statement is built on the assumption that there is indeed no global dimension to world affairs. And to take this view is to look at the world through the lenses of the seventeenth century, when the Westphalian Order called for world affairs to be based on the control of populations, not their protec-

Core Principles of the Responsibility to Protect

- State sovereignty includes the "responsibility to protect" populations from genocide, crimes against humanity, war crimes and ethnic cleansing.

- The "responsibility to protect" embraces the responsibility to prevent and the responsibility to react to such atrocities, as well as the responsibility to rebuild societies shattered by such atrocities.

- The prevention of genocide, crimes against humanity, war crimes and ethnic cleansing should be given priority.

- The international community also has the responsibility to help states protect their populations from genocide, crimes against humanity, war crimes and ethnic cleansing.

- If a state relinquishes its "responsibility to protect"— whether by lack of will or lack of capacity—this responsibility should be borne by the international community that can decide enforcement measures, including the use of force as a last resort.

Richard H. Cooper and Juliette Voinov Kohler,
The 'Responsibility to Protect':
The New Global Moral Compact,
R2P Coalition, 2006. http://r2pcoalition.org.

tion; on the rivalry, not community of states; on exclusion, not integration. But can we live in the 21st century and conduct world affairs based on a vision of the world that is four centuries old? When our very own country did not even exist? Surely no.

We are convinced that there is a relationship between the protection of humans' most basic rights and wider international security, including our own national and personal security. It is unfortunate, but barbaric acts by some too often lead to objectionable behavior by others. Let's not forget the reports of abuses at Guantánamo. War and mass atrocities bring out the evil in us. Let's remember Abu Ghraib. Moral decay may be contagious and those to whom evil is done might do evil in return. The pious pretense that evil does not exist within us, but only within others and that therefore it is of no concern to us, only makes evil vague and menacing. And we quote: "Only among people who think no evil can Evil monstrously flourish." Prudence and self-interest command that we do not ignore hell on earth. Prudence and self-interest forbid us to think that somehow we cannot, will not, be affected by evil.

Those of you who still do not see the necessary connection between us and victims of atrocity crimes cannot seriously remain deaf to prudential arguments based on human and countries' interdependence. We live in a global economy. Events in a distant country may have clear impacts at home. Today we are dependent on the provision of goods that are produced in some countries with weak human rights records. Some think the way forward is to put an end to such relationships before we might suffer from an overnight social uprising with potential mass atrocities that will have impacts on our economy. But this approach—isolationist in nature—will contribute to destroying the delicate web among nations and peoples that we have contributed to build over years, over centuries. And we know that unstable societies, abandoned nations or failed states can be the ultimate refugee for terrorists. Why take the risk, especially when we know far too well the price we then might have to pay.

Prudence and self-interest invite us to cooperate with states and help them build stable societies that will bring out the best in them, and thus the best in us, societies that will not be prone to large-scale horrors, societies that will not be the cradle for breeding terrorists.

Morality

Why should we care about ethics and morality? Because philosophers as ancient as Plato have taught us that ethics provide us with the most sensible and sustainable answers to the question: "How should we live?" Moral guidance is what we seek when we aspire to the best possible human behavior, including when we are dealing with world affairs.

Let us start with the obvious. Today, there is universal acceptance that mass atrocities should not happen. There is no society or culture on Earth that values genocide, crimes against humanity or war crimes. And the immorality of such behaviors was unanimously embraced by world leaders during the 2005 World Summit. This is a field where moral relativism simply does not exist. The basic moral question to be answered is not why we should care for populations that are victims of mass atrocities. This question has already been answered. Rather, what we must ask ourselves is: how should we, the American people, want our country to protect populations from atrocity crimes?

Before turning to this more delicate question, let us summarize the moral case for the doctrine of the "responsibility to protect": why—as world leaders have already agreed— should the international community have the moral and political "responsibility to protect" populations from atrocity crimes?

The answer is that the protection of those going through hell is deeply rooted in empathy, a very deep human feeling. It is no coincidence that all religious traditions impose an obligation of immediate help to a person in need regardless of who she or he is. In the Christian tradition, for example, the classic story of this kind is that of the Good Samaritan.

Mercy, compassion and practical charity all stem from various religions and, together, form a universal moral code. As Elie Wiesel so rightly expressed it as he referred to ongoing mass atrocities: "How can a citizen of a free country not pay attention? How can anyone, anywhere not feel outraged? How can a person, whether religious or secular, not be moved by compassion?"

Indeed, we cannot. But how far should we go?

c) The new global social contract

It is when we talk about the means to prevent or stop mass atrocities, that one realizes how much different countries, different cultures, different societies, different groups, even different individuals will offer differing assessments. Beyond the general framework endorsed by the General Assembly and the requirements adopted by the Security Council, there is no obvious universal code of conduct on how to implement all the facets of the "responsibility to protect." Especially when we ponder over the use of force to protect populations, we enter the realm of moral relativism, political controversy and legal uncertainty. But let's not stop here, because moral relativism is often the refuge of repressive regimes. And, in our quest for moral guidance on how to prevent and stop mass atrocities, let's not succumb to the dangers of moralism:

- moral self-inflation, whereby one instinctively adopts a stance of moral superiority over others and thereby becomes insensitive to the flaws in its own;

- moral oversimplification, whereby outrage acts as a substitute for insight;

- the illicit imposition of values on others.

Let's not allow political controversies stop us. Political will is something that needs to be built. Political consensus is the result of delicately conducted negotiations. Yes, it requires

85

work and the capacity to not only take, but to give. Let's get to work. And finally, let's overcome the current legal uncertainties and build a normative framework based on legitimate, strong and enforceable rules of law.

How does this vision translate itself in concrete steps? In order for our country to exert itself nobly, we need our leaders to pledge to the American people and to all the peoples of the world that our country will protect populations from mass atrocities. This is the first step we must take to abide by the "responsibility to protect": to make this new global social contract a flagship of our country's foreign policy. We must also ask from our leaders that they reclaim collaborative leadership at the global level. The United States must lead in the establishment of effective, legitimate and consistently applied mechanisms—based on the rule of law—to prevent and react to mass atrocities, as well as guide the rebuilding of societies shattered by such atrocities.

The norm of the "responsibility to protect" offers humanity a universal moral and political foundation that compels us to abolish genocide, crimes against humanity and war crimes not only on paper, but on the ground. The norm of the "responsibility to protect" also provides us with a comprehensive approach to reach this goal. Doing so is not only in our hands, it is within our reach.

"Acceding to a set of criteria such as those set forth by the R2P doctrine would be a dangerous and unnecessary step toward bolstering the authority of the United Nations and the international community and would compromise the consent of the American people."

The United States Should Reject the Responsibility to Protect Doctrine

Steven Groves

Steven Groves is a fellow in the Margaret Thatcher Center for Freedom at the Heritage Foundation. In the following viewpoint, he maintains that adopting the Responsibility to Protect (R2P) doctrine would mean that the United States would have an obligation to bear the brunt of humanitarian interventions all over the world. He argues that the doctrine also interferes with U.S. national security.

Steven Groves, "The U.S. Should Reject the UN 'Responsibility to Protect' Doctrine," *Backgrounder* (Heritage Foundation), no. 2130, May 1, 2008. Copyright © 2008 The Heritage Foundation. Reproduced by permission.

As you read, consider the following questions:

1. How did the Proxmire Act define the crime of genocide?

2. According to the author, what is the current position of the United States regarding the R2P doctrine?

3. Why does the author believe that the U.S. military could not operate effectively under the R2P doctrine?

The "Responsibility to Protect" (R2P) doctrine outlines the conditions in which the international community is obligated to intervene in another country, militarily if necessary, to prevent genocide, ethnic cleansing, and other atrocities. Despite its noble goals, the United States should treat the R2P doctrine with extreme caution.

Adopting a doctrine that compels the United States to act to prevent atrocities occurring in other countries would be risky and imprudent. U.S. independence—hard-won by the Founders and successive generations of Americans—would be compromised if the United States consented to be legally bound by the R2P doctrine. The United States needs to preserve its national sovereignty by maintaining a monopoly on the decision to deploy diplomatic pressure, economic sanctions, political coercion, and especially its military forces.

There are ongoing efforts to legitimize the R2P doctrine within the United Nations [UN] and other international forums. The R2P doctrine is being advocated by certain organizations that do not necessarily consider the best interests of the United States as a priority. International organizations such as the United Nations and international nongovernmental organizations (NGOs) such as the World Federalist Movement and the Open Society Institute promote R2P in the interest of a nebulous "international community," not in the interests of the United States or its citizens.

If the United States intervenes in the affairs of another nation, that decision should be based on U.S. national interest, not on any other criteria such as those set forth by the R2P doctrine or any other international "test." . . .

U.S. Policy and the R2P Doctrine

If wholly accepted as official U.S. policy, the R2P doctrine would greatly expand U.S. obligations to prevent acts of genocide around the world. More important, adoption of R2P would effectively cede U.S. national sovereignty and decision-making power over key components of national security and foreign policy and subject them to the whims of the international community.

The U.S. government, as a party to the Convention on the Prevention and Punishment of the Crime of Genocide (the Genocide Convention), is currently obligated to prevent acts of genocide that occur within U.S. territory. The Genocide Convention Implementation Act of 1987 (the Proxmire Act), the legislation implementing the Genocide Convention, was signed into law by President Ronald Reagan in 1988. The Proxmire Act defined the crime of genocide as an act committed "with the specific intent to destroy, in whole or in substantial part, a national, ethnic, racial, or religious group." The new law even criminalized the act of inciting another person to commit an act of genocide. Importantly, U.S. enforcement of these criminal offenses was limited to acts committed in the United States.

However, adoption of the R2P norm would obligate the United States to prevent *all* acts of genocide, ethnic cleansing, and war crimes even if they occur outside of the U.S. Such an obligation would impose unique responsibilities. As the world's preeminent military force, the United States would have to bear a disproportionate share of the R2P international commitment. In the event that acts of genocide and ethnic cleansing occur, the vast majority of nations in the international community could reasonably plead military inferiority on each such occasion, leaving the United States to bear the brunt of any intervention. Most members of the international community could also plead poverty, again leaving the United States to fund the intervention. Even if the intervention is funded through the United Nations system, the United States would still pay an unequal share of the cost.

Current U.S. Policy

The current U.S. position on the R2P doctrine was set forth in a letter from former U.S. ambassador to the United Nations John Bolton to other members of the international community in the run-up to the 2005 World Summit. Ambassador Bolton's letter made it clear that the United States was skeptical of creating a legal obligation requiring one nation to intervene in another:

> [W]e note that the [UN] Charter has never been interpreted as creating a legal obligation for Security Council members to support enforcement action in various cases involving serious breaches of international peace. Accordingly, we believe just as strongly that a determination as to what particular measures to adopt in specific cases cannot be predetermined in the abstract but should remain a decision within the purview of the Security Council.

With reference to the R2P text that was included in the [2005 World Summit] Outcome Document, Ambassador Bolton stated:

> [W]e would like to make changes to make clear that the obligation/responsibility discussed in the text is not of a legal character. . . . We do not accept that either the United Nations as a whole, or the Security Council, or individual states, have an obligation to intervene under international law.

Notwithstanding that position, Ambassador Bolton's letter made the following statement regarding what the United States was willing to commit to in relation to the R2P doctrine:

> For its part, the United States *stands ready to take collective action, in a timely and decisive manner, through the Security Council under Chapter VII of the UN Charter and, as appropriate, in cooperation with relevant regional organizations, should peaceful means be inadequate and national authorities be unwilling or unable to protect their populations.*

The current position of the United States, therefore, is that, while it "stands ready" to take collective action to prevent genocide and ethnic cleansing in another nation, it rejects the notion that it is *legally obligated* to intervene to prevent such atrocities. This position is in harmony with the U.S. commitment in the Outcome Document in which the United States, as a member of the world community, agreed that it was "prepared to take collective action" to protect vulnerable populations. While hardly a renunciation of the R2P doctrine, the current U.S. position falls well short of committing to a legal obligation to act.

Future U.S. Policy

Of course, this is no guarantee that the U.S. position will not change when a new administration comes to power in January 2009. Of the three remaining presidential candidates, all have made statements in favor of humanitarian intervention in general or the R2P doctrine specifically.

For example, when asked in a presidential candidate questionnaire about R2P, Senator Hillary Clinton (D-NY) responded that the United Nations should take steps to "operationalize" the R2P doctrine and stated:

> As president I will adopt a policy that recognizes the prevention of mass atrocities as an important national security interest of the United States, not just a humanitarian goal. I will develop a government-wide strategy to support this policy, including a strategy for working with other leading democracies, the United Nations, and regional organizations.

Senator Barack Obama (D-IL) was more circumspect in his answer to the same questionnaire, stating only that "[t]he Responsibility to Protect is an important and developing concept in international affairs and one which my administration will closely monitor."

Senator John McCain (R-AZ), while not specifically mentioning R2P, has repeatedly stated a willingness to use military force to prevent atrocities in other countries:

I supported humanitarian intervention in order to stop genocide in Kosovo. I wish that the U.S. had acted—with force if necessary—to stop genocide in Rwanda. In neither of these places were America's vital national security interests at stake, though our national values were. Murder in Kosovo and genocide in Rwanda demanded intervention.

Senator McCain also stated:

Africa continues to offer the most compelling case for humanitarian intervention. With respect to the Darfur region of Sudan, I fear that the United States is once again repeating the mistakes it made in Bosnia and Rwanda. . . . My administration will consider the use of all elements of American power to stop the outrageous acts of human destruction that have unfolded there.

While neither Senator McCain nor Senator Clinton has explicitly recognized the existence of a legal obligation to intervene in another country where atrocities are occurring, both have characterized the prevention of genocide as a U.S. national interest, although they apparently disagree on whether or not it constitutes a national *security* interest.

Consider American Interests

While genocide, war crimes, and other atrocities will always be incompatible with American values, the McCain and Clinton statements raise the issue of whether preventing genocide and ethnic cleansing would necessarily constitute a vital U.S. national interest. In some situations, acts of large-scale ethnic cleansing in some remote nation may indeed affect U.S. national interests.

However, the real question is whether or not the United States should obligate itself through an international compact to use its military forces as the rest of the world sees fit in cases of genocide and ethnic cleansing. Accepting such an obligation would arguably empower other nations to judge whether U.S. national interests or national values are at stake. That begs the question of who will decide whether the United States must commit its limited resources—including its military forces—to prevent atrocities occurring in a foreign land. The R2P doctrine is designed to take decision making on these crucial issues out of the hands of the United States and place it in the hands of the international community, operating through the United Nations.

If the United States consented to such a doctrine, it would effectively surrender its authority to exercise an essential, sovereign power.

First Principles and National Sovereignty

The United States must not surrender its independence and sovereignty cavalierly. The Founding Fathers and subsequent generations of Americans paid a high price to achieve America's sovereignty and secure the unalienable rights of U.S. citizens. The government formed by the Founders to safeguard American independence and protect individual rights derives its powers from the consent of the governed, not from any other nation or group of nations.

Having achieved its independence by fighting a costly war, America's Founders approached permanent alliances and foreign entanglements with a fair degree of skepticism. President George Washington, in his 1796 farewell address, favored extending America's commercial relations with other nations but warned against extensive political connections. Washington well understood that legitimate governments are formed only through gaining the consent of the people. He therefore placed a high value on the independence that the United States had achieved and was rightfully dubious about involvement in European intrigues.

Integral to national sovereignty is the right to make authoritative decisions on foreign policy and national resources, particularly the use of the nation's military forces. Many of the reasons why America fought the War of Independence against Great Britain revolved around Britain's taxation of the American people without their consent. . . . Once America gained control of its revenue, natural resources, and industry and had formed a government separate and apart from any other, the Founders would not have compromised or delegated its prerogatives to any other nation or group of nations. Washington rightly warned his countrymen to "steer clear" of such foreign influence and instead to rely on "temporary alliances for extraordinary emergencies."

The Doctrine of National Sovereignty

The R2P doctrine strikes at the heart of the Founders' notion of national sovereignty. The Founders would have deplored the idea that the United States would cede control—any control—of its armed forces to the caprice of the world community without the consent of the American people. Washington stated that the decision to go to war is a key element of national sovereignty that should be exercised at the discretion of the American government:

> Our detached and distant situation invites and enables us to pursue a different course. If we remain one people under an efficient government, the period is not far off . . . when we may choose peace or war, as our interest, guided by justice, shall counsel.

The U.S. interest, guided by justice and exercised with the consent of the American people, must remain the standard for

Considering U.S. National Security

Risking American lives only in situations where America's national security is at stake is neither absolutist nor appealing; it is prudent. What is appealing is the misguided hope that America can serve as the "world's policeman" at every turn to stop competing populations from ripping each other apart, as was the case in Rwanda when the Hutus butchered hundreds of thousands of Tutsis in 1994. What would the average American have said if U.S. forces had intervened in Rwanda and suffered casualties? Probably the same thing they said only a year earlier when they saw the bodies of American soldiers being dragged through the streets of Mogadishu: "What are we doing there?!?"

Steven Groves,
"Should the U.S. Support the UN's
Responsibility to Protect Doctrine?"
Council on Foreign Relations, May 27, 2008. www.cfr.org.

making decisions of war and peace. The interest of the international community, which is guided by its own collective notion of justice and without the consent of the American people, should not serve as America's barometer, especially when placing the lives of U.S. military men and women in jeopardy. The United States cannot rely on world opinion, as expressed through an emerging international norm such as R2P, to set the proper criteria for the use of U.S. military force. The commitment to use force must be made exclusively by the U.S. government acting as an independent, sovereign nation based on its own criteria for military intervention.

In sum, the R2P doctrine does not harmonize with the first principles of the United States. Adopting a doctrine that binds the United States to scores of other nations and dictates how it must act to prevent atrocities is the very sort of foreign entanglement against which Washington warned us. The United States would betray the Founding Fathers' achievement of independence and sovereignty if it wholly acceded to the R2P doctrine.

Additional R2P Impracticalities

In addition to the corrosive effect that the R2P norm, if wholly adopted, would have on U.S. national sovereignty, other aspects of R2P are impractical and collectively fatal to the doctrine.

Under the R2P doctrine, if the United States decides on its own that acts of genocide or ethnic cleansing require intervention, the procedural hoops set forth by the R2P doctrine would prevent the U.S. from acting expeditiously. Additionally, the "precautionary principles" scattered throughout the R2P doctrine would significantly hinder the combat operations of any U.S. armed force ultimately committed to such a mission.

Assignment of Authority to the United Nations

When a crisis or other major world event endangers a U.S. national interest, the United States must have the ability to take action as it sees fit. In the event that the United States determines that atrocities in a foreign land must be stopped, the R2P doctrine would restrict the ability of U.S. armed forces to respond swiftly by requiring the United States to clear a series of barriers and defer to the judgment of multilateral bodies.

Specifically, the R2P doctrine requires the United States or any other nation seeking to end genocide to ask the UN Security Council for permission to intervene. Indeed, the ICISS [International Commission on Intervention and State Sovereignty] report states that the Security Council should be the "first port of call" and that there is "absolutely no doubt that there is no better or more appropriate body than the Security Council to deal with military intervention issues for human protection purposes." The Security Council's failure to act in [the genocides in] Rwanda and Srebrenica—the very situations that gave rise to the ICISS effort—is apparently of little consequence.

Moreover, even if the Security Council fails to act, the R2P doctrine does not free the United States or any other nation to act. Instead, it suggests that authority for military intervention must be sought either from the UN General Assembly or from regional or subregional organizations.

The U.S. national interest—not the UN Security Council, the UN General Assembly, or any other regional organization—should dictate the use of U.S. military force as well as the imposition of economic, political, and diplomatic sanctions. Whether that interest is best pursued through the UN Security Council, through NATO [North Atlantic Treaty Organization], in ad hoc "coalitions of the willing," or completely alone is for the president, the Congress, and the American people to decide. History shows that most nations decide to use their military forces based, first, on their own interests; second, on the interests of their close allies; and last, if at all, on the interests of an undefined "international community." The United States should not submit to a doctrine that would make it the perennial exception to that historical trend.

Operational Flexibility vs. Precautionary Principles

Even if surrendering control of America's armed forces to the will of the world community were acceptable, the U.S. military could not operate effectively under the R2P doctrine.

Once committed to a military operation with all of its attendant risks, U.S. armed forces must be allowed the operational freedom to create the conditions to succeed. However, the R2P doctrine espouses a "proportional means" limitation to the rules of engagement that would likely hinder the success of a military intervention. Specifically, the ICISS report suggests that the "scale, duration and intensity of the planned military intervention should be the minimum necessary to secure the humanitarian objective in question." In other words, any intervening armed force may act only to end genocidal acts and ethnic cleansing—and go no further.

However, a combat environment is rarely so predictable. Some situations would require the total destruction of the forces perpetrating the genocide or the overthrow of the government providing command and control. Yet the ICISS report states that "[t]he effect on the political system of the country targeted should be limited . . . to what is strictly necessary to accomplish the purpose of the intervention." Several instances of genocide and ethnic cleansing in recent history have occurred with the complicity and active involvement of a national government and its armed forces. It is unrealistic to mandate that a military intervention limit its effect on the political system and its leadership while stopping genocidal crimes. It is likewise naïve to believe that government forces that are complicit in genocidal acts would cease and desist from committing atrocities after a military intervention has ended and the intervening troops are withdrawn.

In addition, the R2P doctrine demands that "all the rules of international humanitarian law should be strictly observed" in the event of a military intervention. There is, however, widespread debate over certain crucial aspects of that law. For example, there are major differences of opinion regarding the classification, treatment, confinement, and trial of certain classes of enemy combatants. The use of certain weapons, such as cluster bombs and land mines, is also disputed. The R2P's requirement of strict observance of the law of armed conflict is therefore unachievable because there is broad disagreement on what "strict observance" would entail.

Protecting American Sovereignty

Given the recognition of the Responsibility to Protect doctrine in the 2005 World Summit Outcome Document, as well as the continuing efforts by certain actors in the international community to promote and operationalize R2P, the United States should clarify its position on its national sovereignty and the criteria for the use of its armed forces.

To that end, the United States should:

- Maintain its current official position, as set forth in Ambassador Bolton's letter regarding the 2005 World Summit Outcome Document, that the R2P doctrine does not create a binding legal obligation on the United States to intervene in another nation for any purpose.

- Affirm that the United States need not seek authorization from the UN Security Council, the UN General Assembly, the international community, or any other international organization to use its military forces to prevent acts of genocide, ethnic cleansing, or other atrocities occurring in another country.

- Base its decisions to intervene in the affairs of other nations—including punitive economic, diplomatic, political, and military measures—on U.S. national interests, not on criteria set forth by the R2P doctrine or any other international "test."

- Scrutinize ongoing efforts by certain actors within the international community to operationalize and otherwise promote the R2P doctrine in the United States, the United Nations, the international NGO community, and other international forums.

- Reject the notion that the R2P doctrine is an established international norm.

R2P Should Be Treated with Skepticism

The United States should take no comfort from the fact that, as a party to the 2005 World Summit Outcome Document, it has committed itself only to being "prepared to take collective action" to end atrocities or that the ICISS report represents the obligation to prevent atrocities as a mere "responsibility." R2P advocates are attempting to achieve worldwide consensus that the international community has an obligation to intervene, with military force if necessary, in another country to prevent acts of genocide, ethnic cleansing, and other atrocities. R2P proponents may not be satisfied with anything less than a multilateral treaty—a United Nations Convention on the Responsibility to Protect—that creates binding legal obligations on its signatories.

The United States should therefore continue to treat the Responsibility to Protect doctrine with grave skepticism. The independence won by the Founders and defended by subsequent generations of Americans should not be squandered, but rather should be safeguarded from furtive encroachments by the international community.

Only by maintaining a monopoly on the deployment of diplomatic pressure, economic sanctions, political coercion, and military forces will the United States preserve its national sovereignty. Acceding to a set of criteria such as those set forth by the R2P doctrine would be a dangerous and unnecessary step toward bolstering the authority of the United Nations and the international community and would compromise the consent of the American people.

> "Moving the prisoners to American soil would affirm the startling proposition that we consider ourselves bound by the rule of law."

Terrorists Should Be Incarcerated in U.S. Jails

Steve Chapman

Steve Chapman is a columnist for the Chicago Tribune. *In the following viewpoint, he maintains that incarcerating terrorists in U.S. jails is not a threat to the American public, pointing out that terrorists and other very dangerous criminals reside there already.*

As you read, consider the following questions:

1. How many domestic and international terrorists are already incarcerated in the state of Illinois?

2. According to the author, how many Republican House members from Illinois vehemently object to housing terrorists in Illinois?

3. How many Guantánamo inmates have had to leave for medical treatment?

Steve Chapman, "Terrorists in the Heartland?" *Reason*, December 17, 2009. www.reason .com. Copyright © 2009 Creators.com. By permission Steve Chapman and Creators Syndicate, Inc.

The idea of having an al Qaeda presence in Illinois, even locked up behind bars, is a horrifying prospect. That's what we have to confront now that the [Barack] Obama administration has decided to move some Guantánamo [U.S. detention camp in Cuba] inmates to a prison in Thomson, a small town in the northwest corner of the state. How will we sleep nights with terrorists in our midst?

Probably about like we do right now. From the shrieks of alarm, you'd think no bloodthirsty jihadist had ever occupied a cell in one of our correctional facilities. As it turns out, there are already some 35 domestic and international terrorists privileged to reside in the Land of Lincoln [the state of Illinois].

Run into any at Wal-Mart lately? Seen one cut in line at Dunkin' Donuts? Me neither.

The Sky Has Not Fallen

Just a few weeks ago, a federal judge sentenced Ali al-Marri, a convicted al Qaeda sleeper agent who had undergone terrorist training and met with alleged 9/11 [the terrorist attacks of September 11, 2001] mastermind Khalid Sheikh Mohammed, to eight years behind bars. A former student at Bradley University in Peoria, he is now serving his term at the federal prison in Marion. Yet Illinoisans have somehow stifled their impulse to curl up into the fetal position awaiting certain doom.

A lot of politicians nonetheless insist the risk of relocating detainees to Thomson is intolerable. All seven Republican House members from Illinois vehemently object.

They signed a letter drafted by Rep. Mark Kirk predicting the state would become "ground zero for jihadist terrorist plots, recruitment and radicalization" and insisting that "al Qaeda terrorists should stay where they cannot endanger American citizens."

The U.S. Prison System Is Safe

Being locked up in what will become a supermax prison, however, means they will be in a place where they can no more endanger American citizens than they can party with Paris Hilton. If housing jihadists would provoke attacks here, why hasn't Osama bin Laden carried out massacres in Florence, Colo., whose supermax penitentiary holds several terrorists?

Kirk warns that an inmate who needs more than routine medical care will have to get it at the nearest military hospital, which happens to be in his district—raising all sorts of security risks. Fear not. No inmate has ever left Guantánamo for treatment. The Pentagon says it won't move anyone to Thomson until it ensures the medical unit can "handle all foreseeable detainee health conditions, just as it has done at Guantánamo for the past seven years."

A common theme among Republicans running for senator and governor is that the inmates shouldn't be moved anywhere, because there is no reason to close Guantánamo. Obama's decision, charges Senate candidate Patrick Hughes, is just keeping "a campaign promise to an antiwar, left-wing" faction of his party.

But it's not just Birkenstock-shod peaceniks who support the idea. Former Joint Chiefs of Staff chairman Colin Powell has endorsed it. So has Gen. David Petraeus. Last year, John McCain vowed to close Gitmo [short for Guantánamo] if he became president. There were other presidential candidates who disagreed. You know what? They lost.

The opponents see no risk in keeping Guantánamo open and no gain in getting rid of it. But plenty of military people think the status quo is about as satisfactory as a dead skunk in the living room.

Former Navy General Counsel Alberto Mora told Congress that high-ranking officers "maintain that the first and second identifiable causes of U.S. combat deaths in Iraq—as

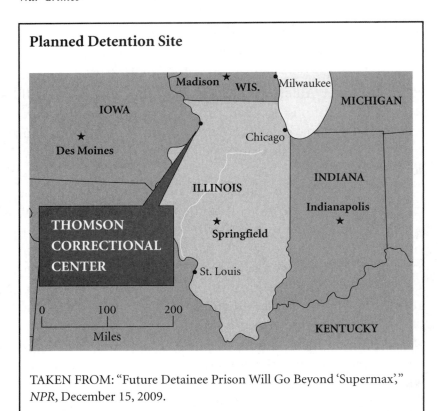

Planned Detention Site

TAKEN FROM: "Future Detainee Prison Will Go Beyond 'Supermax',"
NPR, December 15, 2009.

judged by their effectiveness in recruiting insurgent fighters
into combat—are, respectively, the symbols of Abu Ghraib [a
prison in Iraq] and Guantánamo."

No Lawless Zones

The [George W.] Bush administration's purpose in putting the
captives at the U.S. naval base in Cuba was to keep them beyond the reach of federal courts, so it could do whatever
struck the fancy of [former vice president] Dick Cheney and
[former secretary of defense] Donald Rumsfeld. But the Supreme Court has repeatedly asserted that Guantánamo cannot
be a lawless zone. The executive branch has to follow the Constitution even there.

Moving the prisoners to American soil would affirm the startling proposition that we consider ourselves bound by the rule of law. It wouldn't make veteran terrorists give up the fight. But it would deprive them of an emblem of torture and abuse that inspires anti-American fury and endangers American lives.

When the detainees arrive here, I predict, Illinoisans will pay attention for about five minutes and then go on calmly with their lives. At least the grown-ups will.

VIEWPOINT 4

> "Voluntarily bringing Guantánamo ter-
> rorists into the United States increases
> the chances they will be . . . released
> into the country."

Terrorists Should Not Be Incarcerated in U.S. Jails

John McCormack

John McCormack is the deputy online editor of the Weekly Standard. *In the following viewpoint, he reports on a Republican
congressional memo that criticizes the decision to incarcerate terrorists in Illinois after the prison at Guantánamo Bay is closed.
The Republicans argue that placing terrorists in American jails
will imbue them with more legal protections and will not necessarily make America safer.*

As you read, consider the following questions:

1. What has the Congressional Research Service (CRS) observed about the rights of terrorists?

2. How many members of al Qaeda's leadership cadre
   would be transferred to Illinois?

3. What has been Illinois senator Dick Durbin's position
   on transferring Guantánamo Bay prisoners?

Republicans on the Hill [Capitol Hill, the seat of the U.S.
Congress] are circulating this memo on [President Barack]
Obama's decision to move Gitmo [short for Guantánamo Bay,
a U.S. detention camp in Cuba] detainees to a prison in Illinois:

> Having failed to bring the Olympics to Illinois, President
> Obama will give Illinois an odd replacement gift just in time
> for the holidays—al Qaeda terrorists from the Guantánamo
> detention facility. In announcing this decision, there still re-
> mains no explication of how closing Guantánamo makes
> America safer. Quite to the contrary, unnecessarily import-
> ing al Qaeda terrorists into the United States 1) gives them
> more legal protections, including constitutional rights, than
> they have now at Guantánamo, 2) increases the chances they
> may be released into the country, and 3) in exchange for
> these significant costs, does not appease the Democratic
> base, and certainly will not appease al Qaeda.

Importing Terrorists Likely Gives Them More Legal Protections than They Have Now

It is admittedly unclear precisely what additional legal rights
al Qaeda terrorists gain by their presence inside the United
States, as opposed to their detention at Guantánamo, but the
gain likely is not zero. The Supreme Court has held that "[i]t
is well established that certain constitutional protections available to persons inside the United States are unavailable to
aliens outside of our geographic borders." The Congressional
Research Service (CRS) has observed, "non-citizens held in the
United States may be entitled to more protections under the
Constitution than those detained abroad." When Guantánamo
detainees are moved stateside, they will likely assert broad

protections under the Fifth Amendment Due Process Clause, to cover various conditions and elements of their confinement. They may also raise statutory claims regarding religious practices.

Voluntarily Bringing Guantánamo Terrorists into the United States Increases the Chances They Will Be Released into the Country

One of the most dangerous possibilities related to the transfer of Guantánamo detainees into the United States is that it may give judges the opportunity to order their release into the United States. Where detainees have sought a court order of release into the country, the main case denying that order turned on the fact that the detainees were outside the country. In that case, a Guantánamo terrorist cleared for transfer asked a federal judge last year [2008] to order him released into the United States, which the judge ordered. Thankfully, an appellate judge corrected that error on the grounds that a judge could not order the government to accept someone into the United States from outside the country. It is not clear that the same result obtains once the administration has voluntarily brought Guantánamo detainees into the country.

Even though the president has confidently declared that he will not release detainees into the United States, he may be confronted with a court order directing just that once the administration voluntarily brings al Qaeda terrorists to the United States. The bottom line is, even though Democrats state that President Obama would never release a terrorist into the United States, it is no longer exclusively his choice once he voluntarily brings them here. It makes no sense for the political branches to subcontract to the courts the issue of controlling U.S. borders and administering the admission of aliens, especially enemy aliens.

Creating Guantánamo in Illinois Will Not Appease the Democratic Base

It appears that the Thomson [Illinois] correctional facility will be modified to a level of security that is "beyond supermax." Given this description, it seems highly unlikely that those opposed to the Guantánamo facility will accept law of war detentions of al Qaeda terrorists at another facility other than Guantánamo. For example, Michael Ratner of the Center for Constitutional Rights has characterized the president's detention proposals in the past as "closing Guantánamo physically, but repackaging it" elsewhere. The ACLU [American Civil Liberties Union] of Colorado has called supermax "simply another form of torture."

Creating Guantánamo in Illinois Certainly Will Not Appease al Qaeda

Today's announcement once again raises the canard that closing Guantánamo will remove an al Qaeda recruiting tool, as if al Qaeda would not continue to target the United States for terror attacks once Guantánamo is closed. This argument is belied by all experience with Islamist terrorists, given that the allegedly motivating factor of Guantánamo did not exist at the time of the following:

- 1983: Beirut Marine barracks bombing, killing 241 U.S. Marines

- 1992: approximate beginning of bin Laden's calls to attack United States

- 1993: first World Trade Center attack

- 1995: car bombing at U.S. facility in Riyadh, Saudi Arabia

- 1996: Khobar Towers bombing, killing 19 Americans and wounding 372 others

- 1998: bin Laden issues his "Declaration of War Against the Americans"

- 2000: bombing of USS *Cole* murdering 17 U.S. sailors and injuring 37 others

- 2001: September 11 [2001] terrorist attacks murdering 2,973

So Who Is Coming to Dinner?—Reviewing the Guantánamo Population

It is worth examining the Guantánamo population, part of which is to be moved to the American heartland. Brookings [Institution] assesses the current detainee population to include, according to the government's allegations:

- 26 members of al Qaeda's leadership cadre (or 12 percent of the total population),

- 90 lower-level al Qaeda operatives (or about 41 percent of the total),

- 8 members of the Taliban's leadership cadre (roughly 3.5 percent of the total),

- 81 foreign fighters (or about 37 percent of the total), and

- 11 Taliban fighters and operatives (or about 5 percent of the total).

Another metric finds that 86 detainees, or about 39 percent of the detainee population, admit some degree of affiliation with terrorist organizations, as alleged by the government.

It will be interesting to see if the administration is planning to import into the United States either of these detainees, for example:

© 2009 Gary McCoy, Cagle Cartoons and PoliticalCartoons.com.

- Ghassan Abdallah Ghazi Al Shirbi, who has said, "I'm going to make this easy and short for you guys, . . . I fought against the United States, I took arms. . . . I'm proud of what I did."

- Abdul Ahmed, who said, "I praise the [September 11] attacks. . . . Praise Osama bin Laden. . . . I'm not one of his men and not one of his individuals. I am one of his sons. I will kill myself for him and will also give my family and all of my money to him."

This is in addition to bringing Khalid Sheikh Mohammed and the other leaders of the 9/11 attacks [the terrorist attacks of September 11, 2001] to downtown New York City after they called the military commission charges against them "badges of honor, which we carry with pride," and called themselves "terrorists to the bone."

Hasn't the Senate Clearly Opposed This Move?

Unnecessarily importing al Qaeda terrorists to a prison in Illinois is a direct rebuke of the position once held by the senior senator from Illinois. On July 19, 2007, Senator Durbin joined with Vice President [Joe] Biden [former senator from Delaware], Secretary of State [Hillary] Clinton [former senator from New York], and Secretary of the Interior [Ken] Salazar [former senator from Coloardo] when they were senators in the 94–3 vote in favor of a resolution expressing the position of the Senate that Guantánamo detainees should not "be transferred stateside into facilities in American communities and neighborhoods." More recently, the Senate voted 90–6 to ensure that Guantánamo detainees would not come to the United States when it adopted an amendment to the war supplemental providing that no funds could be used to transfer or incarcerate any Guantánamo detainee to or in the United States. Senator Durbin switched his position to ensure that al Qaeda terrorists could come to Illinois when he voted against this amendment.

Unnecessarily importing al Qaeda terrorists into the United States is also a direct rebuke to the position expressed by the Senate majority leader [Harry Reid] at a press conference on May 19, 2009. When asked if Guantánamo detainees could be imprisoned in the United States, he replied that "part of what we don't want is them to be put in prisons in the United States. We don't want them around the United States." Asked later at the same press conference if he would "be all right with them being transferred to an American prison," the majority leader replied, "not in the United States."

The President Has Not Explained How This Decision Makes America Safer

Voluntarily bringing al Qaeda terrorists into the United States is a fantastically bad idea for multiple reasons, as it clearly fails any cost/benefit analysis. The tremendous costs of this decision include increasing the chances al Qaeda terrorists may be released into the United States, and providing them more legal protections than they currently have at Guantánamo.

Balanced against these enormous costs are an unarticulated set of benefits. Most importantly, it does not seem likely that foreign governments, or the Democratic base for that matter, will cease criticizing the United States for its detention policy once Guantánamo detainees are simply moved to Illinois and law of war detentions continue there. Second, it is surely the case that the removal of this supposed recruiting tool will have zero effect on al Qaeda's continued targeting of the United States for attack. Third, the United States remains engaged in an armed conflict with al Qaeda, which means the United States will still likely be capturing al Qaeda operatives and terrorists for some time. Does today's decision mean that al Qaeda operatives captured in the future will now also be imported into the United States to be given constitutional protections.

> Less than one month ago, Senate Democrats had an opportunity to prevent the wholesale importation of al Qaeda terrorists into the United States, but instead chose to reject an amendment to ensure that federal funds would not be used to modify facilities in the United States to bring Guantánamo detainees here. This vote was twelve days after Senate Democrats rejected another amendment to keep the self-proclaimed mastermind of the September 11 attacks and his cohorts in a military commission. The consequences of these votes became obvious today.

Periodical Bibliography

The following articles have been selected to supplement the diverse views presented in this chapter.

Massimo Calabresi	"Obama Grapples with Holder's 9/11 Trials Plan," *Time*, February 3, 2010.
Jim Comey and Jack Goldsmith	"Holder's Decision on Mohammed Trial Defended," *Washington Post*, November 20, 2009.
Helene Cooper and David Johnston	"Obama Tells Prison to Take Detainees," *New York Times*, December 15, 2009.
Randy James	"A Brief History of Military Commissions," *Time*, May 18, 2009.
Fred Kaplan	"There Are Already 355 Terrorists in American Prisons," *Slate*, May 29, 2009. www.slate.com.
Daniel Klaidman	"Terror Begins at Home," *Newsweek*, February 12, 2010.
Dahlia Lithwick	"Holder Laughed," *Slate*, November 18, 2009. www.slate.com.
Michael B. Mukasey	"Civilian Courts Are No Place to Try Terrorists," *Wall Street Journal*, October 19, 2009.
National Review	"Gitmo by the Lake," December 15, 2009.
Anthony D. Romero	"Terrorists Are Criminals and Should Be Tried in Civilian Court," *U.S. News & World Report*, February 16, 2010.

OPPOSING
VIEWPOINTS®
SERIES

CHAPTER 3

How Should the United States Deal with the ICC?

Chapter Preface

The United States has always had a troubled relationship with the International Criminal Court (ICC). Since the ICC was formally established in 2003 to prosecute war crimes, genocide, and crimes against humanity, American critics of the ICC have made known their wary views of the institution and expressed skepticism that it can be an effective way to implement international justice. They perceive the ICC to be a threat to U.S. sovereignty and a true threat to American national security.

To the ICC's supporters, the opposition of U.S. critics to the court is puzzling. They argue that the court was designed to allow countries to maintain their national sovereignty and ability to police themselves. To many observers, it seems as if the United States doesn't want to play by the rules that were painstakingly established for everyone. If the United States can demand special status, they argue, then what is the point of the rule of law?

American ambivalence to the ICC can be traced back to 2000, when President Bill Clinton signed the Rome Statute of the International Criminal Court. Although he had signed on and stated his support for the aims of the ICC, he announced that he would not be submitting it to the Senate for ratification until it was thoroughly analyzed by U.S. legal and policy experts. When George W. Bush became president in January 2001, he took a hard line with the ICC. His administration sent a note to the secretary-general of the United Nations in May 2002 stating that the United States was suspending its signature and renouncing any obligations to the ICC or the Rome Statute. It was made quite clear that the United States was not going to become a member state.

The administration of President Barack Obama has shifted its stance toward the ICC by signaling a desire to engage the

ICC on a number of levels. During questioning by the U.S. Senate Committee on Foreign Relations prior to her confirmation hearings to become the secretary of state, Hillary Clinton stated that the United States "will end hostility toward the ICC, and look for opportunities to encourage effective ICC action in ways that promote U.S. interests by bringing war criminals to justice." In August 2009, she noted the warming relationship between the Obama administration and the ICC by maintaining that it was a "great regret" that the United States was not a member of the ICC but stated that "we have supported the work of the court and will continue to do so under the Obama administration."

The future of the U.S.-ICC relationship is one of the issues explored in the following chapter of *Opposing Viewpoints: War Crimes*. Other viewpoints examine how engaging the ICC would affect U.S. sovereignty and national security and the implications of politicizing the ICC on international justice and American security concerns.

> *"The benefits of support of the ICC far outweigh the presumed costs, particularly in American credibility and leadership in its foreign policy and its commitment to the rule of law globally."*

The United States Should Engage with the ICC

David Scheffer and John Hutson

David Scheffer is a professor of law and the director of the Center for International Human Rights at Northwestern University School of Law. John Hutson is president and dean of the Franklin Pierce Law Center. In the following viewpoint, excerpted from a report prepared by the Century Foundation, the authors recommend that the United States work on a closer, more cooperative relationship with the International Criminal Court (ICC). Scheffer and Hutson contend that doing so would reaffirm the American commitment to the rule of law and will provide more credibility in U.S. military efforts to bring to justice the leading perpetrators of atrocity crimes.

David Scheffer and John Hutson, *Strategy for U.S. Engagement with the International Criminal Court*, New York, NY: A Century Foundation Report, 2008. Copyright © 2008 The Century Foundation, Inc. All rights reserved. Reproduced by permission.

As you read, consider the following questions:

1. According to public opinion polls, what percentage of Americans support U.S. participation in the ICC?

2. What are the main countries that have not joined the ICC?

3. According to the authors, what is the first step a new president should take to prepare the groundwork for possible ratification of the Rome Statute?

The ICC [International Criminal Court] has aroused neither broad public interest nor outrage among the American people. The ICC has occupied primarily the attention of the fraternity of international lawyers, law professors, and multilateralists supporting the court and some new sovereigntists, military veterans, and conservatives who passionately oppose it as well as many other international institutions. But occasional national polls show that large majorities (ranging from 68 percent to 74 percent) of Americans, when directly asked, support U.S. participation in the ICC. True to form, views on Capitol Hill [the seat of U.S. government in Washington, D.C.] and certainly within the executive branch since 2001 have traded broad public sentiment in support of the ICC for the intense anti-ICC feelings of a few. This might reflect the facts that the ICC barely arose as an issue during the national elections of 2000 or 2004, and that the polling data, though impressive, remain largely hidden from popular discourse.

Nonetheless, external realities have intruded. In recent months, the [George W.] Bush administration has demonstrated a more accommodating spirit. In April 2008, the legal advisor of the State Department, John B. Bellinger III, conceded the reality of the ICC and a willingness to consider "appropriate assistance from the United States in connection with the Darfur matter . . . consistent with applicable U.S. law."

In July 2008, the United States worked hard to draft UN Security Council Resolution 1828, which renewed the mandate of the African Union/United Nations Hybrid operation in Darfur (UNAMID), but then abstained on the vote. The final text of Resolution 1828 includes Russian- and Chinese-inspired language undermining the ICC prosecutor's effort to obtain an arrest warrant against Sudan President Omar Hassan al-Bashir. The United States refused to accept any language designed to weaken the ICC's investigation of Bashir and the Darfur situation. It was a significant turning point for the Bush team. Several years ago the United States had strong-armed the Security Council to include language in peacekeeping renewal resolutions 1422 (2002) and 1487 (2003) in order to immunize American peacekeepers (and others from nations not party to the Rome Statute [the treaty that established the ICC]) from any surrender to the ICC regardless of their conduct on foreign territory.

The ICC Is Beneficial to U.S. Interests

The ICC cannot and must not be ignored. As noxious as it may seem to the cynics, the court is increasingly an important factor in reminding American policy makers of the criticality of the rule of law in shaping U.S. foreign and military policy. We believe that is a much-needed reminder for those who toil in the wake of the Bush legacy. The ICC also offers opportunities to rebuild America's commitment to the pursuit of international justice. But given the Bush administration's deplorable record, particularly regarding detainee abuse and torture during the so-called war on terror since September 11 [2001], the ability of the United States to influence and participate in the global assault on war criminals still hangs in the balance.

The ICC is carving out the future of atrocity law and its enforcement, which has a direct impact on the U.S. military. American lawyers may interpret international humanitarian law and the law of war differently from the ICC judges and, by extension, the growing number of governments that are party to the Rome Statute. The stark reality is that global standards and rules on how to wage armed conflicts will surge ahead without direct U.S. influence. Already, the United States has lost much of its authority on human rights issues and international law on atrocities by being outside the ICC and, during the Bush administration, aggressively opposing it.

The ICC Plays a Key Role

In the four African situations currently falling within the ICC's investigative jurisdiction, peace and justice sometimes compete with each other. The ICC's engagement has to be factored into the likely utility of using economic, political, and military options to confront atrocity crimes and bring stability to parts of Africa of critical concern to the United States. The U.S. government has important global interests in how conflicts in Sudan, Uganda, the Democratic Republic of the Congo, and the Central African Republic are resolved, and the ICC is part of that equation. It is the height of folly to act as if the court has no bearing on these conflicts. This already has been demonstrated by the American involvement in Darfur and the Bush administration's grudging (but critical) support for an active ICC role in that situation.

The ICC has 108 states parties. They include almost every American treaty ally and a large number of countries friendly to the United States. While some of the nations that have joined the ICC have less than stellar records as democratic societies, most of the countries remaining outside of the ICC, with some exceptions, either are autocracies or pay mere lip service to democratic ideals. There are reasons why allies and friends in Europe (including all but two fellow NATO [North Atlantic Treaty Organization] members), Latin America, Africa, Asia, and the Pacific have joined the ICC and consider its benefits both nationally and internationally to far outweigh its potential challenges to their own national interests. Russia, China, Egypt, Indonesia, Turkey, India, Israel, Saudi Arabia, Pakistan, and the United States are the non-ratifying heavyweights. While these certainly are very important nations, including a few American allies, is this really the non-party club (which also includes North Korea, Iran, Cuba, Sudan, Iraq, Syria, Yemen, Zimbabwe, Tunisia, and Myanmar [also known as Burma]) we want to remain with on issues of international justice? Among the non-party nations, the United States has strong military alliances only with Turkey, the Czech Republic, and Israel. In what ways are U.S. values, interests, and concerns regarding international justice more congruent with the views of most of the 84 non-ratifying governments than with those of America's traditional democratic allies and strategic friends among the 108 nations that have joined the ICC? It is significant that Japan, which remains so closely bound to the American defensive shield, might have been expected to toe the American line and oppose the ICC. Yet it acceded to the Rome Statute in 2007. Other states parties include the United Kingdom, Germany, France, Italy, Spain, Poland, Belgium, Ireland, the Nordic and East European countries, Canada, Australia, the Netherlands, Greece, New Zealand, Mexico, Argentina, Colombia, Brazil, South Africa, Nigeria, Botswana, Jordan, and South Korea.

American Explanations Are Falling on Deaf Ears

American conduct in the so-called war on terror has made U.S. rationales for exceptionalism toward, rather than compliance with, international law ring hollow with other governments and publics. American scholars and policy practitioners experience this every time they travel overseas to legal and world affairs conferences and during informal discussions with foreign diplomats. The recitation of U.S. policy on almost any issue of international justice is either politely ignored or openly scorned. American leverage to persuade other nations to interpret the law as we would see it is no longer what it was. Our absence from the ICC only exacerbates the decline in our own influence on the interpretation and application of rules pertaining to the use of military force, detainment and interrogation policies, and the prosecution of perpetrators of atrocity crimes. In this important endeavor, we are no longer a leading nation, nor are we a follower; we are simply an outlier with little international relevance or influence. . . .

A New Administration's Strategy

The new administration, Republican or Democratic, that enters office on January 20, 2009, probably will not exhibit the animus [hostility] toward the ICC that the Bush administration and its allies in Congress have had for so many years. Even if the new administration were to be open to developing a cooperative relationship with the ICC, it likely would not rush toward U.S. ratification of the Rome Statute. There will be many priorities for the new administration, and ratification of the Rome Statute is likely to be regarded even by sympathetic officials as low on the totem pole. However, we believe the critical issues before the 2010 Review Conference [of the Rome Statute] argue strongly in favor of an accelerated path toward U.S. ratification so that our country can participate as a state party in that conference and exercise maximum influence there. We also know that U.S. membership in the ICC would be a significant boost to American credibility and influence throughout the world. Put simply, the ICC really is that important a symbol for other nations of American commitment to the rule of law and human rights.

Whether or not the pace is stepped up, there are some initiatives that even a conservative administration could take to enhance cooperation with the ICC and thus serve the best interests of the United States.

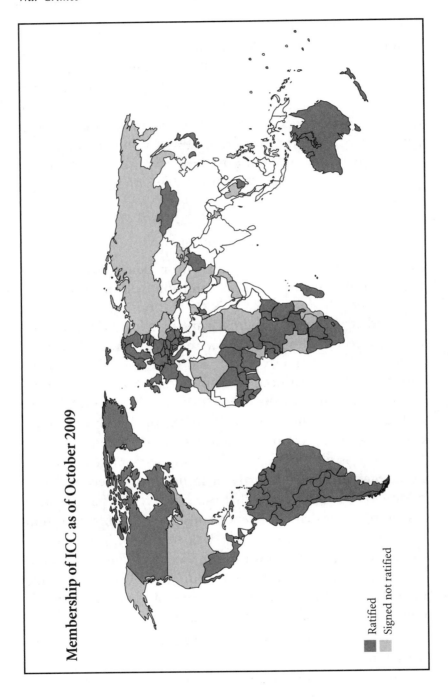

Membership of ICC as of October 2009

Ratified

Signed not ratified

A New Era Leads to New Initiatives

First, *the United States should be more forthright in assisting the ICC with its investigations of atrocity crimes, be they in Africa, Latin America, or elsewhere.* While there are hints of a back-channel link between Washington and The Hague, a more open and transparent relationship should be developed.

Second, *the new president and Congress should repeal certain particularly noxious provisions of the American Service-Members' Protection Act, following up the recent elimination of punitive measures on military aid.* The invasion provision should be the first to go, thus removing that unnecessary irritant in our foreign relations. The president should use his waiver authority under the law more aggressively in order (i) to remove the stain of the remaining economic punitive measures from U.S. relationships with other countries, and (ii) to open up more channels for cooperation with the ICC and thus advance the first initiative stated above. An internationalist president and concerned Congress should recognize that, as the law's primary purposes are to prohibit cooperation on cases with the ICC and to punish nations participating in the ICC, repeal of the entire law would be common sense and do wonders for U.S. credibility overseas.

Third, *the new president and Congress should amend the federal criminal code and the Uniform Code of Military Justice so as to ensure that federal and military prosecutors and courts can investigate and prosecute the full range of atrocity crimes in the Rome Statute.* This will be essential if the United States, even as a non-party to the treaty, is to take full advantage of the complementarity privileges under it. That modernizing process should have high priority in Congress so as to ensure that the United States is not a sanctuary for war criminals. Even the harshest critics of the ICC should see value in shoring up federal and military capabilities in atrocity crimes prosecution so as to always demonstrate U.S. ability-to avoid ICC investigations of Americans regardless of whether the United States joins the Court.

Steps Toward Ratification

A progressively minded new president should take additional steps that would prepare the groundwork for possible ratification.

First, *the next president should convene an advisory group of officials and lawyers from the Departments of Defense (including the Judge Advocate General), State, and Justice, as well as members from the intelligence community, the National Security Council, and key congressional leaders to work through remaining areas of concern and the political and legislative road map for cooperation and possible ratification.* We believe it will be essential for the next president to send a clear signal to the advisory group of his overall intention to seek a constructive and bipartisan pathway to cooperation with the ICC and possible ratification of the Rome Statute. The world has changed since 1998, indeed since 2001, and the next president needs to modernize America's approach to international justice.

Second, *the new president should send a fresh letter to the United Nations informing it that the United States withdraws the letter filed by the Bush administration with the United Nations on May 6, 2002, which deactivated the U.S. signature on the Rome Statute and formally launched the anti-ICC campaign by the Bush team.* The new letter would confirm that the United States henceforth resumes its responsibilities as a signatory state (which primarily means it will not act to undermine the Rome Statute). This would be an easy confidence-building step with our allies and friends that are already committed to the ICC.

Participation in 2010 Review Conference

Third, with steps one and two accomplished, *the new administration should accelerate implementing legislation and plan for ratification in late 2009 or early 2010 so that the United States can participate actively in the forthcoming 2010 Review Conference of the Rome Statute.* The reasons are paramount: States parties will consider the first round of amendments to the Rome Statute, the most important being incorporation of a definition and trigger mechanism for the crime of aggression. U.S. influence is imperative for any consideration of the "crime of all crimes" drawn from the heritage of Nuremberg [the Nuremberg Trials involved German officials charged with war crimes as a result of the Holocaust], which means the new administration should immediately send its representative as an observer to the special working group negotiations on the crime of aggression prior to the Review Conference. If the United States achieves state party status by the time of the Review Conference, then its influence doubtless will be considerable for the final outcome of this significant amendment. Further, as a state party, the United States could weigh in heavily on other critical issues that might be raised at the conference, such as whether or not Article 124 of the Rome Statute, which permits a seven-year opt-out on war crimes charges for any new state party, will be repealed, and whether certain weapons (such as cluster bombs, phosphorous munitions, and anti-personnel land mines) will be added to the treaty as prohibited weapons.

At the Review Conference, the United States, assuming it were to become a state party to the Rome Statute, could press for amendments that should appeal to a broad spectrum of other nations. One amendment could strengthen the complementarity regime by fortifying Article 19(1) of the Rome Statute so as to require ICC judges to undertake an admissibility review immediately prior to surrender of a charged suspect to The Hague [in the Netherlands, seat of the ICC]. Another amendment could add the crime of large-scale corruption in the UN system or among individuals and public agencies on the margins of a UN program (a possibility suggested by the Oil-for-Food Programme scandal) as a prosecutable crime before the ICC.

A third amendment could seek to achieve what many governments, including the United States, had sought in 1998 but
lost to horse-trading tactics at the Rome Conference: adding
as prohibited weapons to the treaty all chemical weapons
identified in the Chemical Weapons Convention [formally the
Convention on the Prohibition of the Development, Produc-
tion, Stockpiling, and Use of Chemical Weapons and on Their
Destruction]. Further, the United States could seek a protocol
to the Rome Statute that would create a highly skilled appre-
hension team that could be deployed to track and arrest fugi-
tives from ICC justice, but only with the prior consent of the
nation(s) where any such fugitive is believed to be hiding.

Benefits Outnumber Risks

The ICC remains a contentious issue in policy circles and a
largely unspoken one among the general public. Therefore,
any strategy that seeks to shift the United States into a closer
relationship with the ICC entails risks and uncertainties that
can be resolved only through a reduction in rhetoric and a
better understanding of the ICC. The benefits of support of
the ICC far outweigh the presumed costs, particularly in
American credibility and leadership in its foreign policy and
its commitment to the rule of law globally. This is especially
true for the U.S. Armed Forces, which have far more to gain
from participating in bringing leading perpetrators of atrocity
crimes to justice than from continued U.S. opposition to the
ICC and absence from its vital work. Maintaining the status
quo would only strengthen the will of atrocity lords to act
with impunity and endanger the lives of U.S. service personnel sent abroad to stop their carnage and restore the peace.

> "Although supporters of the court have a noble purpose, there are a number of reasons to be cautious and concerned about the effect the ICC could have on national sovereignty and politically precarious situations the world over."

The United States Should Reject the Jurisdiction of the ICC

Brett D. Schaefer

Brett D. Schaefer is a research fellow and policy analyst at the Heritage Foundation. In the following viewpoint, he argues that it is a clear violation of international law for the International Criminal Court (ICC) to impose jurisdiction on countries that are not party to the Rome Statute and that the ICC is often undermined by political agendas. Schaefer concludes that the United States should not ratify the Rome Statute and should not recognize its authority over U.S. citizens.

As you read, consider the following questions:

1. According to the author, why was the ICC established?

Brett D. Schaefer, "Crimes Need to Be Punished, But Is the ICC the Right Means?" Heritage Foundation, February 13, 2009. Copyright © 2009 The Heritage Foundation. Reproduced by permission.

2. What are the possible repercussions from the ICC indicting Sudanese president Omar al-Bashir?

3. Why have the United States and several other major countries declined to join the ICC, according to the author?

The International Criminal Court (ICC)—which was formally established in 2003 to prosecute war crimes, crimes against humanity, genocide, and the as-of-yet-undefined crime of aggression—has long held a special place in the hearts of human rights activists and those hoping to hold perpetrators of terrible crimes to account.

Although supporters of the court have a noble purpose, there are a number of reasons to be cautious and concerned about the effect the ICC could have on national sovereignty and politically precarious situations the world over.

One of the most basic principles of international law is that a state cannot be bound by a treaty to which it is not a party. Further, long-standing international legal norms hold that a state cannot be bound to legal assertions that it has specifically rejected. The ICC, however, directly contravenes these norms and precedents of international law; it claims jurisdiction to prosecute and imprison citizens of countries that are not party to the Rome Statute and, more shockingly, over those who have specifically rejected the court's jurisdiction.

Seeking to impose international legal requirements and jurisdiction on unwilling sovereign states is unsupportable, and a clear contravention of international law. It also has significant implications for states that are unable or unwilling to ratify the Rome Statute establishing the ICC.

U.S. Opt-Out

For instance, both the [Bill] Clinton administration and the [George W.] Bush administration concluded that the ICC is a seriously flawed institution that the United States should not join. However, because of the ICC's unprecedented claims of jurisdiction, the United States has had to take unusual steps to protect its citizens and military personnel, including negotiating a network of non-surrender agreements (or Article 98 agreements, after the section of the Rome Statute that permits such arrangements) with as many countries as possible. Countries that sign such agreements with the United States promise, in effect, not to surrender U.S. nationals to the ICC without the consent of the U.S. government.

America pursued Article 98 agreements out of concern that the ICC could be used as a tool by those opposed to its foreign policy to make political statements through ICC prosecutions. Supporters of the ICC disparage this as unnecessary. They claim there are protections in the ICC treaty to prevent abuse of the court—after all, the court can only intervene in cases committed within the territory or involving a citizen of an ICC party, and then only if that country proves unwilling or unable, in the judgment of the court, to investigate and prosecute alleged crimes.

This is cold comfort. Unscrupulous individuals and groups will seek to misuse the ICC for politically motivated attacks, as demonstrated by those urging the court to indict Bush administration officials for alleged crimes in Iraq and Afghanistan. In the first two years of the ICC, more than 100 charges against U.S. citizens were submitted to the court. While the ICC chief prosecutor declined to pursue these cases, there is no assurance that future cases will be similarly resolved.

Because of its relative lack of checks to prevent it from being misused, the ICC represents a dangerous temptation for those with political axes to grind. This is a lesson currently being learned by Israel. Despite the fact that Israel is not a party to the Rome Statute, the ICC prosecutor is reportedly exploring ways to prosecute Israeli commanders for alleged war crimes committed during the recent actions in Gaza.

U.S. Policy Toward the ICC

Since the approval of the Rome Statute, U.S. policy toward the ICC has been clear and consistent: The U.S. opposes the ICC because it is an international legal body
that lacks prudent safeguards against political manipula-
tion, possesses sweeping authority without accountability
to the [United Nations] Security Council, and violates
national sovereignty by claiming jurisdiction over the nationals and military personnel of non-party states.

*Brett D. Schaefer, "The Bush Administration's
Policy on the International Criminal Court Is Correct,"*
Backgrounder *(Heritage Foundation), no. 1830,
March 8, 2005. www.heritage.org.*

Palestinian lawyers argue that Palestine can request ICC
jurisdiction as the de facto sovereign even though it is not an
internationally recognized state. This is a political twofer for
the Palestinians: Pressure is applied to Israel over alleged war
crimes while excluding [Palestinian political organization]
Hamas's incitement of the military action (as well as its war
crimes against Israeli civilians) and, at the same time, momen-
tum is increased for Palestinian statehood without the need to
make compromises with Israel.

Uncompromising Prosecution

The current situation in Sudan raises other issues. Although
the UN [United Nations] Security Council has been largely
deadlocked on possible sanctions against the government of
Sudan for its role in supporting Janjaweed [translated to "evil
on horseback"] militia groups that have committed terrible
crimes in Darfur, it did pass a resolution in 2005 referring the
situation in Darfur to the ICC. This past summer, the ICC an-

nounced that it would seek an indictment against Sudanese president Omar [Hassan] al-Bashir for his alleged involvement in crimes committed in Darfur.

Indicting the sitting head of state of Sudan, no matter how awful his role in the Darfur atrocities may have been, could aggravate the situation in Darfur and put more people at risk. Al-Bashir may decide he has nothing to lose, increase his support of the Janjaweed, and encourage an escalation of their attacks to, possibly, include aid workers and UN and African Union peacekeepers serving in UN missions in Darfur.

If it destabilizes the government, it could also rekindle the north-south conflict that saw roughly 2 million people killed in a 22-year civil war ended by a 2005 peace agreement. These dangers spurred African countries, which would bear the most immediate consequences of a more chaotic Sudan, to call on the UN Security Council to defer the al-Bashir prosecution.

Moreover, since the Office of the Prosecutor is largely autonomous, once a case is brought to the ICC, there is little opportunity to resolve disputes, conflicts, or sensitive political issues diplomatically. For instance, Sudan's neighbors may be faced with the choice of arresting al-Bashir, which could spark conflict with Sudan, or ignoring the court's warrant. If Uganda could resolve its long-festering conflict with the Lord's Resistance Army by agreeing not to prosecute its leader, it would have no ability to call off the ICC prosecution.

It is unlikely the ICC prosecutor or its judges will be held to account if its decisions lead to greater carnage in Darfur, or advancing politically motivated charges in Gaza, or prolonging the conflict in Uganda. They are free to act without considering the potential consequences. Those having to deal with the consequences are not so lucky.

A Credible Court

For these reasons and others, the United States has declined to join the ICC. It is not alone in its concerns as demonstrated by the many states that are not ICC parties. Major countries like China, India, and Russia have refused to ratify the Rome Statute out of concern that it unduly infringes on their foreign- and security-policy decisions—issues rightly reserved to sovereign governments.

Even the [Barack] Obama administration has expressed the need to make sure U.S. troops have "maximum protection" from politically motivated indictments by the ICC and has not rushed to support ratification of the treaty. Do not look for the United States to abandon the Article 98 agreements Washington has signed with some 100 countries around the world anytime soon.

While the ICC embodies an admirable desire to hold criminals accountable for their crimes, the court is flawed notionally and operationally. The more ICC advocates seek to use the court to press political agendas and supersede the prerogatives of government in foreign policy, the more they undermine the credibility of the court and threaten its future as a useful tool for justice.

To protect its own interests and to advance the overarching intent of building a credible international criminal court, the United States should continue to insist that it: is not bound by the Rome Statute because it has not ratified the treaty; will not recognize the authority of the ICC over U.S. citizens or consider joining the court without significant changes to the treaty; and will exercise great care over decisions that support actions of the court in cases like Darfur.

"The heavy-handed tactics of the Bush administration have increased antagonisms and sowed resentment, especially in Latin America."

The United States Should Not Manipulate the ICC

Amitabh Pal

Amitabh Pal is the managing editor of the Progressive. *In the following viewpoint, he condemns recent attempts by the United States to exempt itself from the jurisdiction of the International Criminal Court (ICC). He contends that the United States pressures other countries into signing bilateral agreements that ensure that U.S. personnel would not be sent to the ICC for prosecution.*

As you read, consider the following questions:

1. How many countries have signed bilateral agreements with the United States regarding the ICC?

2. How many countries have refused to sign bilateral agreements with the United States regarding the ICC?

3. According to the author, how much money did Barbados lose in military aid from the United States in 2005 after refusing to sign a bilateral agreement?

For the past four years, the [George W.] Bush administration has systematically set out to exempt the United States from the purview of the International Criminal Court [ICC]. Using bullying tactics, it has often gotten its way. But at a cost.

President Bush's disdain for the International Criminal Court has been clear all along. His administration did everything in its power to sabotage its creation.

Having failed in that effort, it set out to twist the arms of governments the world over to sign bilateral agreements ensuring that they would not send U.S. personnel up to the court for prosecution.

"Our ultimate goal is to conclude [these] agreements with every country in the world, regardless of whether they have signed or ratified the ICC, regardless of whether they intend to in the future," John Bolton, then undersecretary of state for arms control and international security, remarked in 2002.

Today, about 100 countries have abided by the Bush administration's wishes, but more than fifty countries have publicly refused, including two dozen that have lost aid in the process.

Reciprocal Agreements Hinder ICC

These agreements that the Bush administration has been pressuring countries to sign exempt all U.S. citizens—including servicemembers and government officials—from being brought before the International Criminal Court, without a promise that the United States would itself prosecute its citizens for any crimes committed. To maintain a façade of give-and-take, these agreements are often reciprocal.

"Under these agreements, all U.S. nationals and non-nationals employed by the U.S. government must be granted blanket immunity," says Golzar Kheiltash, legal analyst with Citizens for Global Solutions. "So a Kenyan mercenary in Kenya hired by the U.S. government could not be handed over to the ICC."

This diplomatic effort has been run by the State Department at the behest of the White House. . . .

The old Republican Congress passed legislation to punish countries that did not sign on the dotted line, even when doing so undermined other foreign policy goals.

Strong-Arming Countries into Signing

Two major pieces of legislation ensured this. The American Service-Members' Protection Act halts particular kinds of military aid to countries that refused to toe the Bush administration line. And the Nethercutt Amendment cuts off certain types of economic aid for countries unwilling to sign such agreements, including assistance related to disability issues, the promotion of democracy, and the curbing of human trafficking.

"The U.S. administration has pressured states worldwide, including its closest allies, to enter into bilateral agreements, to compel them not to surrender U.S. nationals and persons working for the U.S. government to the ICC," Human Rights Watch stated in December 2005. "Indeed, the United States has threatened to suspend both military and economic assistance for states . . . that refuse to enter into such agreements."

The heavy-handed tactics of the Bush administration have increased antagonisms and sowed resentment, especially in Latin America.

"In my own fifty years' experience of watching U.S.-Latin American relations, I have never known an administration as disliked as this one," says Larry Birns, director of the Council on Hemispheric Affairs.

"The U.S. has had to deploy muscle to achieve its objectives," adds Birns. "It has had to go mano a mano [Spanish for hand to hand] and tell these countries that it is a high priority for the Bush administration that they waive the right to bring U.S. personnel before the International Criminal Court for prosecution."

Countries Rebel Against Washington

Take Costa Rica.

"We may be poor, but we have our dignity," then Costa Rican foreign minister Roberto Tovar said in 2005. He stated that this agreement was "offensive" and that his country would "not undermine the ICC." For its audacity, the country lost more than $400,000 in training aid for its security forces.

Peru was no different.

"Peru will not sign any agreement that impedes it from submitting any country's citizens to the jurisdiction of the International Criminal Court," then foreign minister Manuel Rodríguez remarked in 2004. "Peru rejects pressure from any country on its foreign policy." Peruvian lawmaker Javier Diez Canseco opined that "signing the agreement would represent sacrificing Peru's principles and sovereignty." As a result, Peru has lost $4 million in military funds and is slated to lose as much as $8 million in economic support funds for fiscal year 2006, including money for reforming democracy, combating narco-terrorism, and supporting the country's Truth and Reconciliation Commission.

Ecuador also held off Washington.

"Absolutely no one is going to make me cower," then Ecuadorian president Alfredo Palacio told a television station in June 2005. "Neither the government, nor Alfredo Palacio, nor the Ecuadorian people need to be afraid."

"The U.S. has the democratic right to deny help to nations with which we do not have protection for our military," then U.S. ambassador to Ecuador Kristie Kenney said. But U.S. browbeating of successive Ecuadorian governments had the opposite of the intended effect, uniting the country's politicians against the United States.

Ecuador has lost more than $17 million in military training and is scheduled to lose $7 million in economic assistance in the current fiscal year, including money for democracy building and fighting corruption.

The Bahamas partially buckled.

Then U.S. ambassador to the Bahamas [J.] Richard Blankenship told the country's government in 2003 that if the Bahamas did not sign an agreement, a considerable amount of American aid would be withheld, including assistance for building an airport runway, important to a country heavily dependent on tourism. "You try not ever to be in the position to compromise by coercion on your sovereignty," said Prime Minister Perry Christie. Due to U.S. pressure, the Bahamas has still not ratified the International Criminal Court treaty.

Standing Up for Principles

Nearby, Barbados has stood its ground.

"We will not change our principles for any amount of money," Barbados's then ambassador to the OAS [Organization of American States] Michael King said in 2005. "We're not going to [go] belly-up for $300,000 in training funds." Barbados lost $1.7 million in military aid for fiscal year 2005 as a result of its defiance.

Countries outside of Latin America have also disobeyed Washington.

Public figures and politicians across the board in Kenya condemned U.S. pressure. Kenyan member of parliament Paul Muite said that "America is being utterly immoral" in refusing to join the International Criminal Court and in trying to "blackmail" economically weak countries like Kenya. It "is really very, very insulting to our sovereignty, to our sense of self-respect," Muite added. Kenya has lost $7.8 million in aid, and stands to lose another $15 million in the current fiscal year.

Even before the November elections, there had been noises made both by Democrats and Republicans—including from within the Bush administration itself—that punishing countries for not signing bilateral agreements is hurting the United States. They want to make sure the U.S. military maintains its traditional close ties with countries around the world (ties that have not always served the people of those countries well). The main concern: China is filling the strategic void left by the United States.

Opening a Door for Other Countries

"Decreasing engagement opens the door for competing nations and outside political actors who may not share our democratic principles," General Bantz J. Craddock, head of U.S. Southern Command, testified before Congress in March 2006 in a clear allusion to China.

"We need, perhaps in this committee, to not only sound the alarm, but try to demand or suggest a much more comprehensive approach," affirmed Senator Hillary Clinton. "Because I think that's sending exactly the wrong signal, and it's provided a big opening."

"We have paid a very heavy price in countries where we have cut off these programs for various reasons," Senator John McCain joined in, referring to countries turning toward China for assistance. "And these relationships, obviously, are very vital if we're going to effectively conduct a war on terror."

Even [Secretary of State] Condoleezza Rice separately expressed reservations. On a trip to Puerto Rico, she said that the administration's position was "in a sense, sort of the same as shooting ourselves in the foot." She added, "I think we just have to look at it. And we're certainly reviewing it, and we'll consult with Congress about it."

In early October, Congress passed an amendment to the American Service-Members' Protection Act and Bush issued an executive order waiving the prohibition on military training aid for twenty-one nations, eleven of them in Latin America and the Caribbean.

This "signified recognition on the part of the administration that it was harming itself by the prohibition on training aid," says Kheiltash.

Ending the Coercion

Representative Eliot Engel, Democrat of New York, has introduced a bill to repeal the legislation that coerces countries into signing these bilateral agreements.

"The change in Congress brings high hopes," says Kheiltash. "The new members are less ideological, and we're hoping that the 110th Congress will bring about a total recall of the bilateral agreements campaign."

For some tiny countries, that recall can't come soon enough. Nauru is a dot in the Pacific, but it did not avoid the attention of the State Department.

In February 2003, the nation's then president Bernard Dowiyogo visited Washington, ostensibly to discuss banking reform. At the last moment, U.S. negotiators pulled out the bilateral agreement and pressed for a signature.

"This all took us by surprise, but rather than cause a commotion, President Dowiyogo signed the agreement," Nauru's then ambassador to the UN [United Nations] Vinci Clodumar stated in the *Weekend Australian*. Clodumar subsequently told the paper, "Taking into consideration the sequence of events that led to the signing of the executive order left no doubt in my mind that President Dowiyogo signed the executive order under duress."

When Dowiyogo died a few weeks later, Lincoln P. Bloomfield Jr., then U.S. assistant secretary of state for political-military affairs, eulogized him for "signing an agreement to protect the servicemembers of our countries." Bloomfield added that he was "deeply impressed by the calm determination he showed in pursuing Nauru's interests, despite his weakened condition." Bloomfield concluded: "President Dowiyogo truly died in the line of duty."

Afterward, five Nauruan politicians filed a case in an Australian court alleging that the United States reneged on secret pledges of aid promised to Nauru.

> "I believe that the future of the relation-
> ship between the United States and the
> ICC will be defined mainly by the ex-
> tent to which the United States and
> ICC supporters can agree to disagree
> about the Rome Statute and find con-
> structive and practical ways to work
> together to advance our shared interest
> in promoting international criminal
> justice."

The ICC Must Respect
U.S. National Interests

John B. Bellinger III

*John B. Bellinger III was the legal adviser to the U.S. secretary of
state. In the following viewpoint, excerpted from a speech, he argues that it is the International Criminal Court's (ICC's) responsibility to build a more constructive relationship with the United
States by respecting its national interests and international obligations.*

John B. Bellinger III, "Bellinger's Speech on International Criminal Justice," Council on
Foreign Relations, November 14, 2008. http://www.cfr.org/publication/17777/.

As you read, consider the following questions:

1. What were the Clinton administration's issues with the Rome Statute, according to Bellinger?

2. How have the United States and the ICC cooperated on the issue of Darfur?

3. According to Bellinger, how did ICC supporters overcome their reluctance to create a more constructive relationship with the United States?

[I] turn to the International Criminal Court [ICC], the tribunal which tends to overshadow all the others even though it has yet to try a single case. Of course, in international law circles, the ICC is a hot topic right now. And there is considerable speculation about what the next administration will do with respect to the ICC. I obviously cannot say for sure what will happen on this score, so let me instead describe some aspects of the U.S. approach over the last few years.

It is important to note at the outset that the United States' fundamental concerns about the ICC have been remarkably consistent across successive administrations and Congresses controlled by both Democrats and Republicans. Time will tell if the next administration will take a different approach, but I think it is unlikely, in the absence of significant changes to the Rome Statute [the treaty that established the ICC] to address these concerns, that the United States will become a party to the Rome Statute any time in the foreseeable future. Rather, I believe that the future of the relationship between the United States and the ICC will be defined mainly by the extent to which the United States and ICC supporters can agree to disagree about the Rome Statute and find constructive and practical ways to work together to advance our shared interest in promoting international criminal justice.

Establishing the ICC

While long a proponent of the idea of a permanent international criminal court, during the run-up to the Rome Statute in the 1990s, the United States consistently stressed that establishing an international criminal court was not an end in itself. Rather, we believed, a court's effectiveness would depend on the powers given to the court and the ways in which those powers were integrated into the existing international system for peace and security. In particular, [Bill] Clinton administration representatives at Rome made clear that the ICC must operate in coordination, not in conflict, with the UN [United Nations] Security Council. They opposed proposals to give the court's prosecutor the authority to commence investigations on his or her own initiative, without a referral from the Security Council. They emphasized that the United States and other governments participate together in military alliances and peacekeeping operations around the world, and that the soldiers undertaking these important tasks need to be able to do their jobs without exposure to potentially politicized prosecutions from the court. They also expressed concerns with proposals to have the court exercise jurisdiction over crimes, such as a crime of aggression, which had a very different character than war crimes, genocide, and crimes against humanity.

While U.S. negotiators worked hard to secure agreement on a treaty that would meet these objectives, the negotiations at Rome failed to produce acceptable terms. The concerns the United States made clear at Rome were the basis for President Clinton's decision, announced in December 2000, that the United States would sign the Rome Statute but that he would not submit it to the Senate for advice and consent to ratification. President Clinton stated: "I will not, and do not recommend that my successor submit the treaty to the Senate for advice and consent until our fundamental concerns are satisfied."

My point here is that concerns about the ICC did not begin, and likely will not end, with the present administration [George W. Bush]. Of course, this administration has been criticized for its approach to the ICC, particularly in the first term, when the United States formally notified the UN secretary-general that it did not intend to become a party to the Rome Statute. This has been widely misunderstood as a confrontational U.S. rejection of the ICC. In fact, the central motivation was to resolve any confusion whether, as a matter of treaty law, the United States had residual legal obligations arising from its signature of the Rome Statute not to take steps inconsistent with the treaty's "object and purpose."

The United States Respects the Court

I want to be clear here that it was not the policy of the United States to try to kill the ICC. We have respected the decisions of other states to become parties to the Rome Statute. Under Secretary of State Marc Grossman emphasized this very principle in his 2002 announcement that the United States did not intend to become a party to the Statute. He said: "The United States respects the decision of those nations who have chosen to join the ICC; but they in turn must respect our decision not to join the ICC or place our citizens under the jurisdiction of the court." Our policies have been consistent with this approach—including the so-called "unsigning," and our efforts to secure Article 98 agreements with other states, which were designed to protect U.S. personnel from the jurisdiction of the court, not to interfere with the decisions made by Rome Statute parties to subject their own nationals to the court's jurisdiction.

The concerns, however, that underlay the Clinton administration's actions and the decision in 2002 to inform the UN that the United States did not intend to become a party are still relevant today. They reflect the unique role and interests of the United States as a global military power and as a permanent member of the Security Council, as well as our historically rooted concern that institutional power must be subject to appropriate checks. Even if the next administration decides, despite these concerns, that it would like to pursue having the United States become a party to the Rome Statute, it may be quite difficult to muster support from two-thirds of the Senate. It is important for supporters of the court overseas to appreciate these political realities in the United States.

The ICC and the United States Can Work Together

Still, even if the United States is not a party to the Rome Statute, there are many ways for the United States and ICC parties to work constructively on international criminal justice issues. In recent years, this administration has sought to steer the focus away from unnecessary wrangling over the issues that divide the ICC's supporters and opponents and toward finding practical and constructive ways to cooperate in advancing our common values and our shared commitment to international justice.

We've re-emphasized as a core principle of our policy our respect for the decisions of other states to join the ICC, and have acknowledged that the court can have a valuable role to play in certain cases. On this point, Darfur is exhibit A. In 2005, in one of the first major policy decisions of Secretary [of State] [Condoleezza] Rice's tenure at the State Department, the United States accepted the decision of the UN Security Council to refer the Darfur situation to the ICC. We have said that we want to see the ICC's Darfur work succeed and indicated our willingness to consider an appropriate request for assistance from the ICC in connection with the Darfur matter, consistent with applicable U.S. law. And in recent months, we have opposed efforts by some countries to invoke Article 16 of the ICC Statute to defer the investigation and prosecution of Sudanese President [Omar Hassan] al-Bashir.

The Way Forward

Pushing early toward ratification without a clear view of the [ICC]'s approach ... would be a mistake in policy terms. The political problem is, however, even more acute. Republicans remain deeply skeptical about the Court. Democrats are more favorably disposed. But it is a very serious undertaking to bring a treaty before the Senate for approval. The constitutional requirement of a two-thirds vote is a high hurdle. And if there happened to be as many as 33 senators inclined toward opposition, it is unlikely that any Senate majority leader would be willing to press ahead. This would be especially so if the 67 reflect a lopsided balance between Democrats and Republicans, creating opportunities in partisan electoral politics. And, of course, in the event the vote came up short, the record suggests it could be decades before the Senate would be willing to reconsider the treaty, if at all. At such a time, the Senate's previous rejection would continue to weigh on deliberations.

To get past the partisan considerations, it will be necessary for senators to be far more aware of and comfortable with the workings of the Court than they are now. A U.S. policy of cooperation with the International Criminal Court, pursued carefully over time and accompanied by demonstrable substantive benefits to American interests, may or may not lead to eventual U.S. ratification. But it is the only good path, and perhaps the only path at all, for those who want to go farther.

Tod Lindberg,
"A Way Forward with the International Criminal Court,"
Policy Review (Hoover Institution),
February–March 2010. www.hoover.org.

The irony of the United States' support for the court in opposing an Article 16 deferral is often noted by the press; what I hope will get equal attention is the still-greater irony that some strong supporters of the court seem so willing to consider interfering with the court's prosecution of an individual responsible for genocide. And beyond Darfur, the president has waived restrictions under U.S. law on assistance to a number of countries that had not signed Article 98 agreements with the United States in order to ensure the continuation of important aid to those countries.

ICC Supporters Signal Cooperation

It is now time for ICC supporters to overcome their own reluctance to build a more constructive relationship with the United States. As Under Secretary Grossman said in 2002, "We believe that there is common ground, and ask those nations that have decided to join the Rome Statute to join us there." And, I am glad to say that finally on Monday of this week [November 2008], ICC supporters expressed a willingness to do so. For the first time, after three years of opposition, ICC supporters included language in this year's version of the annual UN General Assembly resolution on the ICC that emphasizes the importance of cooperation by states parties with states that are not parties to the Rome Statute and that notes that the upcoming review conference provides an opportunity to address the concerns of non-parties. This signals, I hope, a new willingness by ICC supporters to stop fighting their ideological battles and trying to convert the United States and instead to cooperate with us and address our legitimate concerns.

For its part, the new administration will no doubt look at a range of issues as it contemplates how best to protect American interests. For example, both the Clinton and Bush administrations have recognized from the outset the risks posed by the possibility of the Rome Statute parties adopting a definition of the crime of aggression that does not meet U.S. red-lines. Much of the work on the definition has been done by a Special Working Group, but that group's work is now coming to an end, with meetings next week—at the meeting of the Assembly of States Parties in The Hague [the seat of government of the Netherlands]—and at the final "resumed sessions" scheduled to take place at the beginning of next year. It is quite unlikely that the Working Group will bridge the very profound differences in points of view about the definition, and the issue will remain unresolved as the parties head toward the Rome Statute Review Conference that is to take place in 2010. With the efforts of the Working Group behind it, the new administration will need to consider how best to position the United States to deal with this important issue going forward. One thing is for certain: If Rome Statute parties adopt an unacceptable definition of the crime of aggression and then amend the Rome Statute so that it applies to non-parties like the United States, they risk triggering a new crisis in their relationship with the United States.

ICC supporters will undoubtedly press the new administration to become parties to the Rome Statute. As I have noted, absent very basic changes to the Rome Statute, the same "fundamental concerns" that led President Clinton to decide not to submit the treaty for ratification will continue to be salient for a new administration and make this, in my view, exceedingly unlikely. The new administration may be pressed to participate as observers in the Assembly of States Parties, to share intelligence and law enforcement information with the ICC, to seek repeal of the American Service-Members' Protection Act, and perhaps even somehow to renounce the "unsigning" of the Rome Statute, and it will be interesting to see how it deals with these issues. The 2010 Review Conference provides an opportunity to address concerns raised by non-parties, and the extent to which ICC supporters constructively use this opportunity can significantly affect the ability of Rome Statute parties and non-parties to work constructively on our shared interests in promoting justice rather than focusing endlessly on our differences about the court.

What Is at Stake

In sum, there are difficult issues ahead for the United States and the ICC, to be sure. But those issues should not cloud the United States' strong and consistent support for international criminal justice—in the former Yugoslavia, in Rwanda, and in Sierra Leone, Cambodia, and Lebanon. Whatever the outcome of the various issues surrounding the ICC, international institutions of criminal justice will continue, in appropriate circumstances, to be important practical tools for ensuring accountability for serious crimes, in particular war crimes, genocide, and other crimes against humanity. We must not forget that that is what is ultimately at stake here: the need to address crimes of the gravest and most heinous nature—crimes that the entire human race condemns. It is an honorable and necessary enterprise, and one the United States fundamentally supports.

Periodical Bibliography

The following articles have been selected to supplement the diverse views presented in this chapter.

John B. Bellinger III — "A Global Court Quandary for the President," *Washington Post*, August 10, 2009.

Jess Bravin — "U.S. Accepts International Criminal Court," *Wall Street Journal*, April 26, 2008.

Thalif Deen — "Aren't There War Criminals in the U.S.?" Inter Press Service, March 9, 2009. www.ips.org.

James A. Goldston — "The International Criminal Court: Justice and Politics," openDemocracy, January 13, 2010. www.opendemocracy.net.

Philip Hammond — "The Tyranny of 'International Justice,'" *spiked*, March 30, 2009. www.spiked-online.com.

David Kaye — "The U.S. Must Reengage with the International Criminal Court," *Los Angeles Times*, March 11, 2009.

Thomas P. Kilgannon — "Obama May Place U.S. Under International Criminal Court," *Human Events*, February 10, 2009.

Josiah Ryan — "Obama Should Move Towards Greater Engagement with International Criminal Court, Former GOP Congressman Says," CNSNews.com, March 30, 2009. www.cnsnews.com.

Brett D. Schaefer and Steven Groves — "The U.S. Should Not Join the International Criminal Court," Heritage Foundation, August 18, 2009. www.heritage.org.

CHAPTER 4

What Governments and Individuals Should Be Tried for War Crimes?

Chapter Preface

For a number of years, the international community has been concerned with stopping the horrible violence being perpetrated on black Muslims in the Darfur region of Sudan, a North African country that has been gripped by civil war for decades. One of the possible legal remedies proposed is using the International Criminal Court (ICC) to investigate and try Sudan's ruling government for genocide, mass rape, and crimes against humanity. The proposal has resulted in controversy, however, as some observers believe that ICC involvement will not be effective and will lead to more violence and chaos in an already devastated region.

The most recent wave of conflict in Darfur can be traced back to February 2003 when two rebel groups, the Sudan Liberation Movement/Army (SLM/A) and the Justice and Equality Movement (JEM), took up arms to fight against the Arab-controlled Sudanese government. Accusing Sudanese officials of favoring Arabs and oppressing black Africans, rebel forces began a campaign to address inequities through violence against government officials. An Arab militia quickly formed to counter the rebel groups. Known as the Janjaweed, this militia was made up of members of Arab nomadic tribes from the northern regions of the country. Allegedly backed by the Sudanese government, the Janjaweed rampaged through Darfur, engaging in genocide, mass rape, and brutal attacks on men, women, and children. The subsequent fighting between the Janjaweed and rebel groups in Darfur displaced millions of people, forcing many of them to escape to neighboring Chad. Hundreds of thousands of Sudanese are dead as a result of the fighting.

In the face of such shocking violence, the international community began to respond. In September 2004, U.S. Secretary of State Colin Powell classified the conflict in Darfur as genocide, deeming it the worst humanitarian crisis of the twenty-first century. After a series of attempts to deal with the problem, the United Nations Security Council formally referred it to the ICC in March 2005. Two years later, the ICC issued arrest warrants against Ahmed Haroun, the former minister of state for the interior, and Ali Kushayb, a top Janjaweed leader. In response, the Sudanese government stated that the ICC had no jurisdiction over Sudanese citizens; therefore, the ICC arrest warrants meant nothing and the men would not be turned over for trial.

More controversy erupted when the ICC filed charges of war crimes against President Omar Hassan al-Bashir, accusing him of masterminding a plan to commit genocide against three tribal groups in Darfur. In March 2009, a warrant for his arrest was issued. Although the ICC found that there wasn't enough evidence to charge him with the specific intent to commit genocide, he will be charged with war crimes. So far, al-Bashir remains a free man, as Sudan continues to reject the jurisdiction of the ICC.

The situation with Omar al-Bashir and other Sudanese officials is debated in the following chapter, which explores governments or individuals who should be tried for war crimes by the ICC. Other viewpoints examine conflicts in Israel and George W. Bush administration officials who authorized torture and the possibility of the ICC trying them for war crimes.

> "To date, too little mention has been
> made of investigations that show there
> is sufficient evidence to bring charges of
> war crimes and crimes against human-
> ity against Israel's political and mili-
> tary leadership for their actions in
> Gaza."

Israel Should Be Tried for War Crimes Against Gaza

John Dugard

*John Dugard is a professor of law, a former United Nations spe-
cial rapporteur on human rights in the Occupied Palestinian
Territories, and the chairman of the Independent Fact Finding
Committee on Gaza. In the following viewpoint, he argues that
enough evidence exists to try the country of Israel for war crimes
for its actions in Gaza in 2006, when Israeli forces bombarded
and invaded Gaza in response to Palestinian rocket attacks.*

As you read, consider the following questions:

1. What did the UN investigation into attacks carried out
   by the Israel Defense Forces (IDF) show?

2. What did the Independent Fact Finding Committee (IFFC) report conclude?

3. According to the IFFC, how many Palestinian civilians did the IDF kill?

President [Barack] Obama's recent speech to the Muslim world failed to address allegations that Israel committed war crimes in Gaza. Palestinians and people throughout the region were shocked at the firepower Israel brought to bear against Gaza's civilians and do not want Palestinians' ongoing misery to be further ignored. Many were surely waiting to hear from President Obama that the way to peace does not lie through the devastation of civilian life and infrastructure in Gaza.

Two Reports Document War Crimes

To date, too little mention has been made of investigations that show there is sufficient evidence to bring charges of war crimes and crimes against humanity against Israel's political and military leadership for their actions in Gaza. Recently, two comprehensive independent reports have been published on Gaza, and earlier this month [June 2009] a mission mandated by the UN [United Nations] Human Rights Council, and chaired by South African Richard Goldstone, visited Gaza to conduct a further investigation into Israel's offensive.

On May 4 [2009], the United Nations published the findings of an investigation into attacks carried out by the Israel Defense Forces (IDF) on UN premises in Gaza. Led by Ian Martin, formerly head of Amnesty International, this investigation found Israel responsible for wrongfully killing and injuring Palestinians on UN premises and destroying property amounting to over $10 million in value. Although this investigation did not address the question of individual criminal responsibility, it is clear that the identified wrongful acts by Israel constituted serious war crimes.

On May 7, the Arab League [officially the League of Arab States] published the 254-page report of an Independent Fact Finding Committee (IFFC) it had established to examine the legal implications of Israel's Gaza offensive. This committee, comprising six experts in international law, criminal law and forensic medicine from non-Arab countries, visited Gaza in February. We concluded that the IDF had committed serious war crimes and crimes against humanity.

Disturbing Accounts

As the committee's chairman, I spent five days in Gaza along with the other experts. Our views were deeply influenced by interviews we conducted with victims and by the evidence of destruction of property. We were particularly disturbed by the accounts of cold-blooded killings of civilians committed by some members of the IDF and the Israeli military's use of white phosphorus in densely populated areas. The devastation was appalling and raised profound doubts in my mind as to the veracity of Israeli officials who claimed this was not a war against the Palestinian people.

The IFFC found that the IDF, in killing some 1,400 Palestinians (at least 850 of whom were civilians), wounding over 5,000 and destroying over 3,000 homes and other buildings, had failed to discriminate between civilian and military targets, terrorized civilians, destroyed property in a wanton manner not justified by military necessity and attacked hospitals and ambulances. It also found that the systematic and widespread killing, injuring and terrorizing of the civilian population of Gaza constituted a crime against humanity.

Did Israel Commit Genocide?

The IFFC investigated the question whether the IDF was responsible for committing the 'crime of crimes'—genocide. Here we concluded that although the evidence pointed in this

Excerpt from the Report of the UN Fact-Finding Mission on the Gaza Conflict

After reviewing Israel's system of investigation and prosecution of serious violations of human rights and humanitarian law, in particular of suspected war crimes and crimes against humanity, the [UN Fact-Finding] Mission found major structural flaws that in its view make the system inconsistent with international standards. With military "operational debriefings" at the core of the system, there is the absence of any effective and impartial investigation mechanism and victims of such alleged violations are deprived of any effective or prompt remedy. Furthermore, such investigations being internal to the Israeli military authority, do not comply with international standards of independence and impartiality. The Mission believes that the few investigations conducted by the Israeli authorities on alleged serious violations of international human rights and humanitarian law and, in particular, alleged war crimes, in the context of the military operations in Gaza between 27 December 2008 and 18 January 2009, are affected by the defects in the system, have been unduly delayed despite the gravity of the allegations, and, therefore, lack the required credibility and conformity with international standards. The Mission is concerned that investigations of relatively less serious violations that the GOI [Government of Israel] claims to be investigating have also been unduly protracted.

Human Rights in Palestine
and Other Occupied Arab Territories,
Report of the United Nations Fact-Finding
Mission on the Gaza Conflict, *September 15, 2009.*

159

direction, Israel lacked the intention to destroy the people of Gaza, which must be proved for the crime of genocide. Instead, the IFFC found that the purpose of the offensive was collective punishment aimed at reducing the population to a state of submission. However, the IFFC did not discount the possibility that individual soldiers had acted with the required genocidal intent.

Israel's argument that it acted in self-defense was rejected, *inter alia* [among other things], on the basis of evidence that Israel's action was premeditated and not an immediate response to rockets fired by militants and was, moreover, disproportionate. The IFFC found that the IDF's own internal investigation into allegations of irregularities, which exonerated the IDF, was unconvincing because it was not conducted by an independent body and failed to consider Palestinian evidence.

Palestinian Militants Also Guilty

The IFFC also examined the actions of Palestinian militants who fired rockets indiscriminately into southern Israel. We concluded that these actions constituted war crimes and that those responsible committed the war crimes of indiscriminate attacks on civilians and the killing, wounding and terrorization of civilians.

The past twenty years have brought important developments in international law in respect to accountability for international crimes. Yet Israel has possibly secured impunity for itself by failing to become a party to the Rome Statute of the International Criminal Court. Nevertheless, its actions may still be judged by the court of public opinion.

A bold Obama speech on Gaza would have ensured that the public is on notice that it's not business as usual in Washington. Even American allies, such as Israel, should have to answer evidence of serious international crimes. In this way, some measure of accountability may be achieved. With an ac-

What Governments and Individuals Should Be Tried for War Crimes?

tive American push, a new view of the United States may begin to take shape after eight years of disregard for international and domestic law.

161

"Mr. Goldstone's recommendation [in the Goldstone Report] to convoke the International Criminal Court is like putting a loaded pistol to Israel's head—or, in the future, to America's."

Israeli Attacks on Gaza Are Not War Crimes

John Bolton

John Bolton is a senior fellow at the American Enterprise Institute. In the following viewpoint, he attacks the Goldstone Report (formally known as the Report of the United Nations Fact-Finding Mission on the Gaza Conflict *and headed by former South African judge Richard Goldstone), which concludes that Israel's military campaign against the Palestinian group Hamas was "actually aimed against Gaza's citizens as a whole." Bolton concludes that the recommendation that Israel's actions be prosecuted by the International Criminal Court (ICC) as a war crime sets an unfortunate precedent for countries just trying to defend themselves against terrorists.*

As you read, consider the following questions:

1. Why did the United States vote against establishing and joining the Human Rights Council (HRC) of the United Nations (UN)?

2. According to the author, how did the Obama administration react to the Goldstone Report?

3. How many of the HRC's 47 members voted against the resolution endorsing the Goldstone Report's recommendations?

The UN's Human Rights Council (HRC) voted overwhelmingly on Friday to endorse the recommendations of the lopsidedly anti-Israel Goldstone Report [formally the *Report of the United Nations Fact-Finding Mission on the Gaza Conflict*]. The report, named for former South African judge Richard Goldstone, who chaired the underlying investigation, concluded that Israel's 2008–2009 military campaign against the terrorist group Hamas was actually aimed against Gaza's residents as a whole. Thus it was an illegitimate exercise of "collective punishment," an extraordinarily amorphous legal concept.

Fighting Terrorism Is a Crime?

The report alleges numerous specific human rights violations by both Israel and Hamas. But by attempting to criminalize Israel's strategy of crippling Hamas, the report in effect declared the entire antiterrorism campaign to be a war crime. Mr. Goldstone recommended that Israel and the Palestinians should each conduct their own investigations, failing which the [United Nations] Security Council should refer the entire matter to the International Criminal Court for possible prosecution.

In the month since the report's release, it has roiled the Middle East peace process. An Israeli spokesman said "it will

Israeli Response to the Goldstone Report

The Military Advocate General ended his opinion on the five special command investigations by underlining the IDF's [Israel Defense Forces'] commitment to compliance with the Law of Armed Conflict, as well as its intention to investigate thoroughly every alleged violation by IDF forces. He noted that the evidence gathered by the special investigations reflected great effort by the IDF to ensure such compliance and to minimize harm to civilians.

The Military Advocate General acknowledged that the investigations had found operational lapses and errors in the exercise of discretion. However, given the complexities of decision making under pressure, particularly when the adversary has entrenched itself within the civilian population, such mistakes do not in themselves establish a violation of the Law of Armed Conflict.

Israel Ministry of Foreign Affairs,
Gaza Operation Investigations: An Update,
January 2010.

make it impossible for us to take any risks for the sake of peace," perhaps foreshadowing Israeli withdrawal from negotiations while the report remains under active UN consideration.

A Biased Report

The HRC resolution endorsing the report's recommendations repeatedly lacerated Israel, leading Mr. Goldstone himself to cringe, saying he was "saddened" the resolution contained "not a single phrase condemning Hamas as we have done in the report." A U.S. State Department spokesman conceded that the adopted text "went beyond even the scope of the Goldstone Report itself."

The UN General Assembly created the HRC on March 15, 2006, to replace the discredited Human Rights Commission, which had spent much of its final years concentrating on Israel and the U.S. rather than the world's real human rights violators. The [George W.] Bush administration voted against establishing this body and declined to join it, believing, correctly, that it would not be an improvement over its predecessor. President Barack Obama changed course, and the U.S. won election to the HRC in May [2009]. Mr. Obama argued that engagement would be more effective than shunning the HRC and attempting to delegitimize it.

The Goldstone Report thus provides a stark test of Mr. Obama's analysis. Predictably, the administration blamed the report's underlying mandate and its stridently anti-Israel tilt on America's earlier absence from the HRC when the investigation was authorized and launched. Yet the new administration's diplomacy had no discernible impact on the HRC's disgraceful resolution.

How Countries Voted

Twenty-five of the HRC's 47 members voted for the resolution (including Russia and China), six voted against (Hungary, Italy, the Netherlands, Slovakia, Ukraine and the U.S.), and 11 abstained (Japan, South Korea and several European governments among them).

Five didn't vote at all, including Great Britain and France. Press reports indicated that London saw its inaction as a "favor" to Israel, a position simultaneously inexplicable and gutless. It is hard to know just how much real politicking the Obama administration did before this vote, but the loss of key allies is telling.

Implications of the Goldstone Report

The Goldstone Report has important implications for America. In the UN, Israel frequently serves as a surrogate target in lieu of the U.S., particularly concerning the use of military force preemptively or in self-defense. Accordingly, UN decisions on ostensibly Israel-specific issues can lay a predicate for subsequent action against, or efforts to constrain, the U.S. Mr. Goldstone's recommendation to convoke the International Criminal Court is like putting a loaded pistol to Israel's head— or, in the future, to America's.

Mr. Obama has now met the new HRC, same as the old HRC, thus producing a "teachable moment," a phrase he often uses. Quasi-religious faith in "engagement" and the UN has run into empirical reality. When the administration picks itself up off the ground, it should become more cognizant of that organization's moral and political limitations.

Although it will be hard for Mr. Obama to swallow, the logical response to Friday's debacle is to withdraw from and defund the HRC. Otherwise the Goldstone Report will merely be the beginning, next time perhaps with Washington as its unmistakable target.

> "The ICC warrant provides an opportunity to change the rules, holding [Sudanese president Omar Hassan] al-Bashir personally responsible for achieving massive improvements, or personally responsible for committing massive crimes."

Sudan's Leaders Should Be Tried for War Crimes in the ICC

Michael J. Gerson

Michael J. Gerson is a columnist for the Washington Post, *a fellow at the Council on Foreign Relations, and a senior research fellow at the Institute for Global Engagement's Center on Faith & International Affairs. In the following viewpoint, he asserts that traditional diplomacy to bring Sudanese leaders—particularly President Omar Hassan al-Bashir—to justice have failed, therefore the International Criminal Court's (ICC's) issuing of a warrant for his arrest signals a renewed attempt to force a solution.*

As you read, consider the following questions:

1. Why was the author once skeptical of the usefulness of ICC indictments?

2. Why has the author changed his mind on the ICC getting involved?

3. According to the author, what should be al-Bashir's only hope of self-preservation?

While a new administration is just getting started, history doesn't stop.

On Sudan and Darfur, President [Barack] Obama's Africa team has begun a lengthy policy review and is mulling names for a special envoy. But an arrest warrant for Sudanese President Omar Hassan al-Bashir on charges of war crimes and crimes against humanity was reportedly approved by the International Criminal Court (ICC) this week [February 2009]. And the administration suddenly faces an unprecedented question: Can a hunted war criminal also be a partner in the Sudan peace process?

Mixed Feelings on the ICC

While in government, I was skeptical of the usefulness of ICC indictments in situations such as Sudan. Indictments are a blunt diplomatic instrument—once imposed, they are almost impossible to withdraw in exchange for concessions. They leave a thug in a corner—less likely to negotiate and more likely to lash out at humanitarian groups and civilians. A dictator with no options is dangerous.

But I have changed my mind in the case of al-Bashir. The traditional carrots and sticks of diplomacy have failed. For decades, the Sudanese regime has been masterful at using minor concessions and delaying tactics, playing allies who want oil and critics with short attention spans, to achieve its genocidal ends. Al-Bashir would like nothing better than to play another

© 2008 Nate Beeler, The Washington Examiner, and PoliticalCartoons.com.

round in this game. The ICC warrant provides an opportunity to change the rules, holding al-Bashir personally responsible for achieving massive improvements, or personally responsible for committing massive crimes.

International Reactions

There are three predictable international reactions to the ICC arrest warrant against al-Bashir.

1. Sudan's traditional enablers—China, the Arab League [officially the League of Arab States], South Africa and other nations of the African Union—will push the UN [United Nations] Security Council to defer enforcement. Sudan's current negotiations in Doha with Darfur rebels may result in apparent progress, including a rough framework for future peace talks. Supporters of Sudan will argue that this is reason enough to give al-Bashir a reprieve and some breathing room.

2. Britain and France, in contrast, will probably insist on the enforcement of the warrant to maintain the institutional credibility of the ICC.

3. The United States can be expected to take a different approach. For a variety of reasons—particularly the strong military objection to having soldiers tried by foreign courts—the United States has not joined the ICC and is not likely to do so during the Obama administration. The focus of American policy has been on negotiating a positive outcome in Darfur with Sudan's government, not defending the institutional health of the ICC.

Resolving the Problem

But progress in Darfur now requires the ICC warrant to mean something. Granting a deferral in exchange for another round of worthless Sudanese pledges and promises would be the surrender of international seriousness. Al-Bashir's only hope of self-preservation should be the achievement of large changes on the ground in Sudan—a verified cease-fire mechanism in Darfur supported by the international community; the implementation of resettlement and compensation; an end to all harassment of humanitarian groups; full compliance with the Comprehensive Peace Agreement between Sudan's north and south and with all other international commitments.

> "The ICC has no jurisdiction in Sudan because that nation is not a party to the ICC and the alleged crimes are occurring in Sudan and being committed by Sudanese people."

Sudan's Leaders Should Not Be Tried for War Crimes in the ICC

Brett D. Schaefer

Brett D. Schaefer is a fellow in the Center for International Trade and Economics at the Heritage Foundation. In the following viewpoint, he contends that a regional ad hoc tribunal established by the United Nations Security Council is a better solution to the problem of trying Sudanese war criminals than the International Criminal Court.

As you read, consider the following questions:

1. How many people have died in Darfur as of 2005?

2. How much money has the United States contributed in humanitarian aid to the Darfur region?

Brett D. Schaefer, "Why the U.S. Is Right to Support an Ad Hoc Tribunal for Darfur," *WebMemo* (The Heritage Foundation), no. 665, February 15, 2005. Copyright © 2009 The Heritage Foundation. Reproduced by permission.

3. What does the author cite as the first priority in regard to Darfur?

The United States and many advocates of the International Criminal Court (ICC) have long been at odds over the structure, autonomy, and jurisdiction of the court. While these differences have not been resolved, the U.S. opposition to a United Nations [UN] Security Council resolution referring the situation in Darfur region of Sudan to the ICC has rekindled international and domestic attention on America's policy toward the ICC.

Proponents of the ICC argue that the court is the best option to investigate allegations of war crimes, human rights violations, and possible genocide in Darfur. The United States instead has advocated a regional ad hoc tribunal established by the Security Council charged with specifically addressing the situation. As with earlier disagreements over U.S. policy toward the ICC, advocates of the court seek to portray the U.S. position as shortsighted and at odds with human rights.

Nothing, however, could be further from the truth. The U.S. position is one based on accountable government, respect for sovereignty, and a desire for local resolution of problems.

U.S. Efforts to Stop Atrocities in Darfur

The crisis in Darfur began in 2003 when two rebel groups challenged the authority of the Islamist government in Khartoum. The rebel groups claimed that the government was discriminating against the African ethnic groups in favor of nomadic Arab ethnic groups. The resulting conflict quickly escalated: Over 70,000 people have died, and 1.8 million have fled to refugee camps in Sudan and neighboring Chad. Numerous reports allege rampant atrocities committed by the Arab "Janjaweed" [translated as "evil on horseback"] militia groups against non-Arab villagers with the support of the Khartoum government.

The United States has been leading the effort to stop the atrocities in Darfur. While serving as secretary of state, Colin Powell declared that violations of human rights, war crimes, and genocide are occurring. The United States led the effort to pass a Security Council resolution condemning the atrocities and has pressed for economic sanctions on Sudan because of the government's support for militia groups committing atrocities in Darfur. The United States has been a key supporter of the African Union peacekeepers authorized by the Security Council to monitor the situation, in addition to being the largest donor of humanitarian aid to the region, providing nearly $550 million since 2003.

The United States has been frustrated in its effort. The Security Council has not imposed sanctions because China, France, and Russia, afraid that their commercial interests would suffer, have threatened to veto resolutions imposing sanctions. The United Nations Human Rights Commission [replaced by the UN Human Rights Council in 2006] has minimized criticism of Sudan because that nation sits on the Commission. And ICC advocates have focused attention away from the true failure—the inability to get a Security Council resolution imposing sanctions if Sudan fails to constrain the Janjaweed—onto U.S. opposition to a Security Council resolution requesting that the ICC investigate atrocities in Darfur.

Why the ICC Is Not the Best Option

The ICC has no jurisdiction in Sudan because that nation is not a party to the ICC and the alleged crimes are occurring in Sudan and being committed by Sudanese people. Therefore, advocates of the ICC are urging the Security Council to refer the case to the court by way of Article 13 (b) of the Rome Statute [the treaty that established the ICC]. The UN commission investigating abuses committed in Darfur offers a useful summary of the arguments on why the Security Council should refer the case to the court. These arguments are not convincing.

1. The investigation and prosecution of crimes perpetrated contributes to peace and stability by removing obstacles to national reconciliation and peace. Investigation and prosecution of those responsible for crimes is important, but pursuit of justice must be tempered by the need to end atrocities. The immunity offered to [former self-appointed Chilean president] General Augusto Pinochet paved the way for democracy in Chile. The national reconciliation process in South Africa has proven successful. While this paper is not advocating such an option for Darfur, alternative means for removing despots or resolving conflicts should not be dismissed in all cases—especially if heedless pursuit of justice makes peace or transition to democracy more difficult.

2. Trials in The Hague [the seat of the ICC in the Netherlands] might ensure a neutral atmosphere and be less likely to stir up political passions. Using the ICC would undermine ongoing efforts to build regional capacity among Africans to handle conflicts and hold those who commit atrocities to account. As noted by international lawyers Lee Casey and David Rivkin [Jr.], "both of the ICC's current investigations involve African countries, the Democratic Republic of [the] Congo and Uganda, respectively. Adding Darfur to this list begins to look a very great deal like European justice for African defendants."

3. Only the authority of the ICC, backed by that of the United Nations Security Council, might compel both Sudanese government and rebel leaders to submit to investigation and possible criminal proceedings. The Security Council possesses the authority, jurisdiction, and enforcement capacity necessary to compel cooperation in Sudan. As a party to the United Nations Charter, Sudan must abide by decisions of the council. The Security Council can grant authority to the ICC, but could just as easily grant it to an ad hoc tribunal. The ICC has no jurisdiction in Sudan and by itself brings no authority to the table.

The Danger of Pursuing al-Bashir

The Sudan Government [headed by President Omar Hassan al-Bashir] sees the ICC as the gravest threat to its survival it has ever faced and a matter of life and death. It is a national issue, not one confined to Darfur. Up to now, the Sudan Government has responded coolly to the threat, but it is clear that no option is off the table should an arrest warrant be issued.

Alex de Waal, "Dangerous Weeks Ahead,"
Making Sense of Sudan Blog, Social Science Research Council,
January 25, 2009. http://blogs.ssrc.org/sudan.

4. The ICC, with an entirely international composition and a set of well-defined rules of procedure and evidence, is best suited to ensuring a veritably fair trial. The ICC possesses characteristics that would not be deemed "fair" by most Americans, including the possibility of double jeopardy, absentee trials, inability to confront witnesses testifying against the defendant, permissibility of hearsay evidence, and other usages not permitted in American courts. Nor is the ICC international in the sense that all nations support it. On the contrary, only half the nations of the world are parties to the ICC. An ad hoc tribunal approved by the Security Council would be international in composition—indeed, would be universal as the Security Council compels compliance by all UN member states—and could adopt any rules deemed appropriate including the ICC's rules of evidence and procedure.

5. The ICC could be activated immediately, without any delay. The ICC could indeed decide to investigate, but an ad hoc tribunal would be directed to investigate. Both would suffer from necessary delay. For instance, the ICC prosecutor received referrals to investigate alleged crimes in Uganda and

the Democratic Republic of the Congo on January 1, 2004, and April 19, 2004, respectively. The prosecutor took six months to open an investigation in Uganda, took more months to designate judges, and still has not prosecuted anyone a year later. The decision on Congo took two months, with similar delays on judges and prosecutions. An ad hoc tribunal based on the existing infrastructure of the International Criminal Tribunal for Rwanda would reduce delay in establishing an ad hoc tribunal and could count on support from African states.

6. The institution of criminal proceedings before the ICC, at the request of the Security Council, would not necessarily involve a significant financial burden for the international community. This is doubtful. The International Criminal Tribunal for the former Yugoslavia (ICTY) had a staff of 1,238 as of January 2004 and a budget of $135.9 million, and the International Criminal Tribunal for Rwanda (ICTR) had a staff of 1,042 and a budget of $125.6 million. By comparison, the draft ICC budget for 2005 estimates a staff of 526 and a budget of $89.6 million. Expenses for staff account for 57 percent of the draft ICC budget, or $97,095 per staff member. Budget expenditures on staff at the ICTY and the ICTR are 58 percent and 68 percent, respectively, or about $69,372 per staff member at ICTY and $77,279 per staff member at ICTR. Thus, a considerable amount of saving gained through a permanent staff working multiple cases will be lost through higher staff costs. Moreover, the budgets of the ICTY and ICTR increased swiftly in the early years as they began investigations and trials. Since the ICC has barely begun to investigate the current cases in Uganda and Congo, its budget will likely increase substantially over the next few years as the ICC begins to fully investigate, collect evidence, make arrests, and conduct trials. While the United States is not a party to the ICC and cannot be assessed for these expenses, it is likely that the ICC will request funds from the UN if the Security Council refers a case to the body.

The bottom line is that, while the United States is opposed to a Security Council resolution supporting an ICC investigation in Darfur, it also has proposed a credible—perhaps superior—alternative for holding perpetrators of crimes to account.

Establish Priorities Regarding Sudan

The United States has been a leader in trying to force the Sudanese government to stop its support of the militia groups committing atrocities in Sudan's Darfur region. The failure of the Security Council to impose sanctions on the Sudanese government despite the best efforts of the U.S. government is a tragedy that sadly reveals the failures of the UN in dealing with human rights abuses. Unfortunately, ICC advocates have focused attention away from the true failure onto U.S. opposition to the ICC. In truth, the United States fully supports the idea of a tribunal to address allegations of war crimes, human rights abuses, and genocide.

As important as it is to bring those responsible for the atrocities in Darfur to account, the first priority must be to stop the killing. If supporters of the ICC spent a fraction of the energy consumed by criticizing the United States on trying to pressure China, France, and Russia to support a strong Security Council resolution imposing sanctions on Sudan if the Sudanese government continues to support militia groups and authorizing a peacekeeping force charged with protecting the people in Darfur, they would do far more good for those suffering in Darfur.

"*We cannot continue a war on terrorism while being violators of international law ourselves.*"

Bush Administration Officials Who Authorized Torture Should Be Tried for War Crimes in the ICC

Jonathan Turley

Jonathan Turley is a professor of law at the George Washington University Law School. In the following viewpoint, he argues that by authorizing the use of waterboarding, the United States is guilty of war crimes. He concludes that by shielding those who perpetrated war crimes from prosecution, the United States is violating international law and destroying its credibility in the war on terror.

As you read, consider the following questions:

1. When did the U.S. military use waterboarding in the Philippines?

2. What happened to the perpetrator of that torture, Major Edwin F. Glenn?

3. What does the Convention Against Torture expressly state about torture?

For many people around the world, it is a sign of the decline of American moral leadership that we continue to debate whether the government should prosecute those involved in the [George W.] Bush torture program. Their confusion is understandable. Under our existing treaty obligations, we agreed to prosecute such crimes, and we have prosecuted others for precisely the same acts for decades. The real question should be: Should the United States violate international law to shield individuals accused of war crimes? Our answer to that question will define or redefine this country for generations.

Notably, in the past few months, the many law professors who once defended the torture program have largely disappeared. The shrinking number of apologists for the Bush administration is left with largely political arguments in the face of three unassailable legal truths. First, waterboarding is torture. Second, torture is a war crime. Third, the United States is obligated to prosecute war crimes.

Debate About Waterboarding

Despite early spin, there has never been a true debate about the status of waterboarding as torture. It has been a well-recognized form of torture since before the Spanish Inquisition. Indeed, it has remained popular because it leaves no incriminating marks and requires little training or equipment. It was the chosen form of torture of the [German Nazi secret police] Gestapo, [Canadian Communist leader] Pol Pot, and the Bush administration.

The status of waterboarding as torture was established by the United States. The U.S. military used waterboarding ("the water cure") in the Philippines in 1898. While the accused insisted (as do many today) that the torture was justified under the necessities and law of war, members of Congress rejected the argument and demanded the prosecution of Maj. Edwin F. Glenn. He was court-martialed and convicted of the crime of torture.

The United States remained a moral leader on torture for decades, including our prosecution of Japanese officers for waterboarding American and Allied soldiers. One, Yukio Asano, was sentenced to 15 years of hard labor for waterboarding.

In 1983, the Justice Department prosecuted and convicted James Parker, a sheriff in Texas, and his deputies for waterboarding a prisoner. Parker was sentenced to four years in prison.

Did the United States Use Torture?

Legal experts around the world have denounced the Bush program as classic and clear torture. They have been joined by interrogators and officials from the Bush administration itself, including various Bush administration lawyers who vehemently objected to torture at the time.

Susan J. Crawford, a former judge and convening authority for the Bush military tribunals, and State Department official Richard Armitage acknowledged that we tortured individuals. Republican John McCain (himself a victim of torture) has called it torture. President Obama and Attorney General Eric Holder declared that waterboarding is torture. Leading organizations like the International Red Cross define it as not just torture but a war crime.

Torture Is a War Crime

That brings us to the second truth: Torture is a war crime. This one is easy, and even the dwindling number of George W. Bush apologists do not seriously question this point. Torture is a crime under domestic and international law. Various federal laws address torture, not the least of which is the Torture Act, 18 U.S.C. § 2340. There is also the Convention Against Torture and Other Cruel, Inhuman, or Degrading Treatment or Punishment, which President Reagan signed. The Convention Against Torture expressly states that "just following orders" is no defense and that "no exceptional circumstances whatsoever" will be considered. This is acknowledged as a binding law, including recently by former secretary of state Condoleezza Rice.

Finally, the United States is obligated to investigate and prosecute war crimes. Under the Convention Against Torture, we agreed to make "all acts of torture offenses under [our] criminal law" and to prosecute any such cases. The failure to prosecute war crimes committed by your own government is an offense of the same order as the original war crime.

Bush was adamant on the prosecution of war crimes in other countries. In 2003, he insisted, "War crimes will be prosecuted, war criminals will be punished, and it will be no defense to say, 'I was just following orders.'" On June 26, 2003, conservatives applauded as Bush told the United Nations that the United States "is committed to the worldwide elimination of torture, and we are leading this fight by example."

Our failure to investigate and prosecute accused war criminals has led some United Nations officials to accuse the United States of violating treaty obligations. More important, our continued debate over this question puts our troops in danger. We will be hard-pressed in the future to call for prosecution of leaders who torture our citizens and soldiers.

The United States Cannot Shield War Criminals

We cannot continue a war on terrorism while being violators of international law ourselves. Torture and terrorism are cut from the same legal bolt: Both are violations of human rights and international law. If we want the world to join us in fighting one crime against humanity, we cannot continue to obstruct the prosecution of another crime against humanity.

Ultimately, we all become accessories after the fact if we stand silent in the face of these war crimes. Bush ordered these war crimes because he believed that he was above the law, and others like Rice have claimed that, if the president orders such actions, they are by definition legal. They were both wrong. The law is clear. The only remaining question is whether we have the national character and commitment to the rule of law to hold even our leaders to account for crimes committed in our name.

Such prosecutions do not weaken a nation. They reaffirm the difference between ourselves and those we are fighting. To abandon our principles for politics would be to hand al Qaeda its greatest victory: not the destruction of lives or buildings but our own self-inflicted wound of hypocrisy and immorality. True victory against our enemies will be found only on the other side of prosecuting those who (like our enemies) claim the right to wage war by any means.

> "Transnationalists from outside and, now, inside our government have been ardent supporters of prosecutions against American officials who designed and carried out the Bush counterterrorism policies that kept this country safe after 9/11."

Bush Administration Officials Are Not Guilty of War Crimes

Andrew C. McCarthy

Andrew C. McCarthy is an attorney and columnist for the National Review *and* Commentary. *In the following viewpoint, he asserts that enhanced interrogation techniques fall "woefully short of torture crimes under federal law." Therefore, McCarthy concludes, any prosecution of George W. Bush administration officials who crafted antiterrorism policies would be nothing other than political in nature.*

As you read, consider the following questions:

1. According to the author, what is the definition of "transnationalism"?

2. What does McCarthy believe is on Harold Koh's agenda?

3. What is the doctrine of "customary international law"?

"This is an administration [of Barack Obama] that is determined to conduct itself by the rule of law. And to the extent that we receive lawful requests from an appropriately created court, we would obviously respond to it."

It was springtime in Berlin and [U.S. attorney general] Eric Holder, a well-known "rule of law" devotee, was speaking to the German press. He'd been asked if his Justice Department would cooperate with efforts by foreign or international tribunals to prosecute U.S. government officials who carried out the [George W.] Bush administration's post-9/11 [the terrorist attacks of September 11, 2001] counterterrorism policies. The attorney general assured listeners that he was certainly open to being helpful. "Obviously," he said, "we would look at any request that would come from a court in any country and see how and whether we should comply with it."

What Holder Really Meant

As the Associated Press reported at the time, Holder was "pressed on whether that meant the United States would cooperate with a foreign court prosecuting Bush administration officials." He skirted the question in a way Americans ought to find alarming. The attorney general indicated that he was speaking only about "evidentiary requests." Translation: The Obama administration will not make arrests and hand current or former American government officials over for foreign trials, but if the Europeans or UN [United Nations] functionaries (at the nudging of, say, the Organisation of the Islamic Conference) want Justice's help gathering evidence in order to build triable cases—count us in.

Hue and cry followed Holder's decision this week [August 2009] to have a prosecutor investigate CIA [Central Intelligence Agency] interrogators and contractors. The probe is a nakedly political, banana republic–style criminalizing of policy differences and political rivalry. The abuse allegations said to have stunned the attorney general into acting are outlined in a stale CIA inspector general's [IG's] report. Though only released this week—a disclosure timed to divert attention from reports that showed the CIA's efforts yielded lifesaving intelligence—the IG report is actually five years old. Its allegations not only have been long known to the leaders of both parties in Congress, they were thoroughly investigated by professional prosecutors—not political appointees. Those prosecutors decided not to file charges, except in one case that ended in an acquittal. . . . The abuse in question falls woefully short of torture crimes under federal law.

Americans are scratching their heads: Why would Holder retrace this well-worn ground when intimidating our intelligence-gatherers so obviously damages national security? The political fallout, too, is palpable. Leon Panetta, the outraged CIA director, is reportedly pondering resignation. President Obama, laying low in the tall grass on his Martha's Vineyard vacation, is having staffers try to put distance between himself and his attorney general. It is unlikely that many will be fooled: Both Obama and Holder promised their antiwar base just this sort of "reckoning" during the 2008 campaign. But the question remains, Why is Holder (or, rather, why are Holder and the White House) instigating this controversy?

The Doctrine of Transnationalism

I believe the explanation lies in the Obama administration's fondness for transnationalism, a doctrine of post-sovereign globalism in which America is seen as owing its principal allegiance to the international legal order rather than to our own Constitution and national interests.

Recall that the president chose to install former Yale Law School dean Harold Koh as his State Department's legal adviser. Koh is the country's leading proponent of transnationalism. He is now a major player in the administration's deliberations over international law and cooperation. Naturally, membership in the International Criminal Court [ICC], which the United States has resisted joining, is high on Koh's agenda. The ICC claims worldwide jurisdiction, even over nations that do not ratify its enabling treaty, notwithstanding that sovereign consent to jurisdiction is a bedrock principle of international law.

Concerns About the ICC

As a result, there have always been serious concerns that the ICC could investigate and try to indict American political, military, and intelligence officials for actions taken in defense of our country. Here it's crucial to bear in mind that the United States (or at least the pre-Obama United States) has not seen eye to eye with Europe on significant national security matters. European nations, for example, have accepted the 1977 Protocol I to the Geneva Conventions, while the United States has rejected it. Protocol I extends protections to terrorists and imposes an exacting legal regime on combat operations, relying on such concepts as "proportional" use of force and rigorous distinction between military and civilian targets. That is, Protocol I potentially converts traditional combat operations into war crimes. Similarly, though the United States accepted the torture provisions of the UN Convention Against Torture [and Other Cruel, Inhuman or Degrading Treatment or Punishment] (UNCAT), our nation rejected the UNCAT's placing of "cruel, inhuman, and degrading treatment" on a par with torture. By contrast, Europe generally accepts the UNCAT in toto [completely].

As long as we haven't ratified a couple of bad human rights treaties, why should we care that Europe considers them binding? Because of the monstrosity known as "customary international law," of which Koh is a major proponent. This theory holds that once new legal principles gain broad acceptance among nations and international organizations, they somehow transmogrify into binding law, even for nations that haven't agreed to them. That is, the judgment of the "international community" (meaning, the judgment of left-wing academics and human rights activists who hold sway at the UN and the European Union) supersedes the standards our citizens have adopted democratically. It is standard fare among transnational progressives to claim that Protocol I is now binding on the United States and that what they define as cruel, inhuman, and degrading treatment is "tantamount to torture."

Universal Jurisdiction

And the transnational Left has still another treat in store: its notion of "universal jurisdiction." This theory holds that individual nations have the power to prosecute actions that occur in other countries, even when they have no impact on the prosecuting nation. The idea is that some offenses—such as torture and war crimes—so offend the purported consensus of humanity (i.e., so offend left-wing sensibilities) that they may be prosecuted by any country that cares to take the initiative. In fact, many countries (the United States included) open their justice systems to civil suits against government officials—again, even if the country where the suit is filed has nothing to do with the alleged offenses.

So we come back to Holder in Berlin. Two months before the attorney general's visit, the UN's "special rapporteur on torture" told German television that the Obama administration had "a clear obligation" under the UNCAT to file torture charges against former president George W. Bush and former defense secretary Donald Rumsfeld. The rapporteur was relying on documents produced because of American investigations—including a nakedly partisan report by the Democrat-controlled Senate Armed Services Committee.

Meanwhile, . . . Spain's universal-justice crusader Baltasar Garzón is pursuing his own torture case against Bush administration lawyers who weighed in on interrogation policy. Garzón is the Spanish investigating magistrate who, with the help of a terrorist turned human rights lawyer, had Chilean strongman Augusto Pinochet arrested in England for crimes against humanity. The same terrorist-lawyer, Gonzalo Boye, is helping Garzón on the Bush case. The Brits, by the way, eventually decided not to send Pinochet to Spain, but not before the law lords ruled that they could, a decision enthusiastically hailed at the time by UN High Commissioner for Human Rights Mary Robinson, the former president of Ireland. . . .

Working Against U.S. Interests

And then there is the Center for Constitutional Rights [CCR], a Marxist organization that for years has coordinated legal representation for terrorists detained at Guantánamo Bay [U.S. detention center in Cuba]. The CCR has been attempting to convince Germany, France, Spain, and other countries to file war-crime indictments against former Bush administration officials, including President Bush, Vice President [Dick] Cheney, and Secretary Rumsfeld. In representing America's enemies, CCR has collaborated with many private lawyers, who also volunteered their services—several of whom are now working in the Obama Justice Department. Indeed, Holder's former firm boasts that it still represents 16 Gitmo [short for Guantánamo] detainees (the number was previously higher). And, for help shaping detainee policy, Holder recently hired Jennifer Daskal for DOJ's [the Department of Justice's] National Security Division—a lawyer from Human Rights Watch with no prior prosecutorial experience, whose main qualification seems to be the startling advocacy she has done for enemy combatants.

Put it all together and it's really not that hard to figure out what is going on here.

The Way Forward

Transnationalists from outside and, now, inside our government have been ardent supporters of prosecutions against American officials who designed and carried out the Bush counterterrorism policies that kept this country safe after 9/11. The UN's top torture monitor is demanding legal action, almost certainly as a prelude to calling for action by an international tribunal—such as the ICC—if the Justice Department fails to indict. Meantime, law enforcement authorities in Spain and elsewhere are weighing charges against the same U.S. officials, spurred on by the CCR and human rights groups that now have friends in high American places. In foreign and international courts, the terrorist-friendly legal standards preferred by Europe and the UN would make convictions easier to obtain and civil suits easier to win.

Obama and Holder were principal advocates for a "reckoning" against Bush officials during the 2008 campaign. They realize, though, that their administration would be mortally wounded if Justice were actually to file formal charges—this week's announcement of an investigation against the CIA provoked howls, but that's nothing compared to the public reaction indictments would cause. Nevertheless, Obama and Holder are under intense pressure from the hard Left, to which they made reckless promises, and from the international community they embrace.

A Reckoning to Come

The way out of this dilemma is clear. Though it won't file indictments against the CIA agents and Bush officials it is probing, the Justice Department will continue conducting investigations and releasing reports containing new disclosures of information. The churn of new disclosures will be used by lawyers for the detainees to continue pressing the UN and the Europeans to file charges. The European nations and/or international tribunals will make formal requests to the Obama administration to have the Justice Department assist them in securing evidence. Holder will piously announce that the "rule of law" requires him to cooperate with these "lawful requests" from "appropriately created courts." Finally, the international and/or foreign courts will file criminal charges against American officials.

Foreign charges would result in the issuance of international arrest warrants. They won't be executed in the United States—even this administration is probably not brazen enough to try that. But the warrants will go out to police agencies all over the world. If the indicted American officials want to travel outside the United States, they will need to worry about the possibility of arrest, detention, and transfer to third countries for prosecution. Have a look at this 2007 interview of CCR president Michael Ratner. See how he brags that his European gambit is "making the world smaller" for Rumsfeld—creating a hostile legal climate in which a former U.S. defense secretary may have to avoid, for instance, attending conferences in NATO [North Atlantic Treaty Organization] countries.

The Left will get its reckoning. Obama and Holder will be able to take credit with their supporters for making it happen. But because the administration's allies in the antiwar bar and the international Left will do the dirty work of getting charges filed, the American media will help Obama avoid domestic political accountability. Meanwhile, Americans who sought to protect our nation from barbarians will be harassed and framed as war criminals. And protecting the United States will have become an actionable violation of international law.

I'm betting that's the plan.

Periodical Bibliography

The following articles have been selected to supplement the diverse views presented in this chapter.

Steve Bloomfield	"Waiting for the Court," *Newsweek*, January 16, 2009.
Sam Dealey	"Omar al-Bashir: Sudan's Wanted Man," *Time*, August 13, 2009.
Christopher Dickey	"What Would Jesus Do in Gaza?" *Newsweek*, December 24, 2009.
Randy James	"Sudanese President Omar Hassan al-Bashir," *Time*, March 5, 2009.
Brett Joshpe	"It Isn't About the Middle East Conflict," *American Spectator*, October 5, 2009.
Tony Karon	"U.N. War Crimes Allegation Won't Change Israel's Calculation," *Time*, September 17, 2009.
Russell Mokhiber	"Prosecuting Bush for War Crimes," *CounterPunch*, February 25, 2010.
Paul Moorcraft	"Bashing Omar al-Bashir," *American Spectator*, May 29, 2009.
Paul Stares and Alexander Noyes	"Think Twice on Bashir," *Newsweek*, March 5, 2009.
Warren P. Strobel	"General Who Probed Abu Ghraib Says Bush Officials Committed War Crimes," McClatchy Newspapers, June 18, 2008.
Nick Wadhams	"Indicted over Darfur, Sudan's President Feints and Punches Back," *Time*, October 21, 2008.

For Further Discussion

Chapter 1

1. In their viewpoint, David B. Rivkin Jr. and Lee A. Casey assert that terrorists should be treated like enemy combatants and war criminals. In a counterpoint, Wesley K. Clark and Kal Raustiala argue that terrorists should be considered criminals and tried in civilian court. In your opinion, how should the United States treat terrorists? Explain your answer.

2. Private security firms such as Blackwater have garnered controversy for their actions in Iraq. Human Rights First maintains that when Blackwater breaks the law in Iraq, the responsible personnel should be treated as war criminals. Others such as George H. Wittman argue that the allegations against Blackwater are political in nature and are not based on the reality of life in occupied Iraq. How do you think Blackwater should be treated in light of the contrasting opinions presented in these viewpoints?

3. Should Somali pirates be treated as war criminals? Read the supporting and dissenting viewpoints of John Yoo and Jeremy Scahill to inform your opinion.

4. The use of mass rape as a weapon has been documented in Darfur and the Democratic Republic of the Congo. Alyson Zureick contends that perpetrators should be treated as war criminals, while Binaifer Nowrojee points out that rapists are rarely tried as war criminals, despite the rhetoric surrounding the issue. After reading both viewpoints, how serious do you think the international community is about getting tough with rapists? Do you think this should be a top priority of the international justice community?

Chapter 2

1. Richard H. Cooper and Juliette Voinov Kohler maintain that it is within the best interests of the United States to embrace the Responsibility to Protect doctrine. Steven Groves argues that the United States should reject it. With which viewpoint do you agree and why?

2. Should terrorists be incarcerated in American jails? In his viewpoint, Steve Chapman presents reasons why they should. John McCormack reports reasons why the Republican Party believes that terrorists should not be placed in American jails. Which viewpoint is more persuasive?

Chapter 3

1. Should the United States engage with the International Criminal Court (ICC)? David Scheffer and John Hutson believe that it is within the best interests of the United States to engage with the ICC. Brett D. Schaefer believes otherwise. With which viewpoint do you agree and why?

Chapter 4

1. Should Israel be tried for war crimes in the ICC? John Dugard maintains that Israel's actions in Gaza meet the criteria for war crimes. John Bolton counters by arguing that they do not. Which argument is more persuasive?

2. In his viewpoint, Michael J. Gerson lays out his case for trying Sudan's leaders for war crimes in the ICC, while Brett D. Schaefer maintains that the ICC is the wrong venue for legal proceedings. Do you think the ICC should try Sudan's leaders for war crimes? Why or why not?

3. Whether the George W. Bush administration is guilty of war crimes for authorizing torture has been as very controversial issue. Jonathan Turley contends that members of the Bush administration should be tried for war crimes. Andrew C. McCarthy vehemently disagrees, finding politi-

cal motives have led to such charges. Do you agree with McCarthy that charges of war crimes are politically motivated, or is it plausible that the Bush administration may be guilty of war crimes by authorizing torture?

Organizations to Contact

The editors have compiled the following list of organizations concerned with the issues debated in this book. The descriptions are derived from materials provided by the organizations. All have publications or information available for interested readers. The list was compiled on the date of publication of the present volume; the information provided here may change. Be aware that many organizations take several weeks or longer to respond to inquiries, so allow as much time as possible.

American Society of International Law (ASIL)
2223 Massachusetts Avenue NW, Washington, DC   20008
(202) 939-2000 • fax: (202) 797-7133
Web site: www.asil.org

The American Society of International Law (ASIL) was founded in 1906 to "foster the study of international law and to promote the establishment and maintenance of international relations on the basis of law and justice." It is a nonprofit, nonpartisan organization that holds seminars, meetings, and classes on international law for attorneys, corporate counsels, academics, students, judges, diplomats, government bureaucrats, and employees of international organizations. ASIL publishes a number of online and print newsletters and publications, such as *ASIL Insights*, *IL Post*, *International Law in Brief*, and the *ASIL Newsletter*. It also publishes a range of books on international law and legal issues.

The American Non-Governmental Organizations Coalition for the International Criminal Court (AMICC)
801 Second Avenue, 2nd Floor, New York, NY   10017-4706
(212) 907-1357 • fax: (212) 682-9185
e-mail: amicc@amicc.org
Web site:www.amicc.org

The American Non-Governmental Organizations Coalition for the International Criminal Court (AMICC) is a coalition of nongovernmental organizations working to ensure that the United States will ratify the Rome Statute and thereby join the International Criminal Court (ICC). The AMICC promotes grassroots support of the ICC, including creating and supporting alliances between bar associations, women's groups, human rights organizations, religious organizations, veterans' groups, victims' organizations, and student groups to help them utilize the ICC to further their institutional goals. Part of that mission is education: The AMICC disseminates information on how the ICC can help American citizens and groups get justice on an international scale and lobby politicians and bureaucrats on the benefits of fully engaging the ICC. The AMICC holds a series of seminars, lectures, and panel discussions to that end. It also publishes a number of fact sheets, reports, and in-depth studies on ICC investigations and issues related to the court.

Amnesty International (AI)
5 Penn Plaza, New York, NY   10001
(212) 807-8400 • fax: (212) 627-1451
e-mail: aimember@aiusa.org
Web site: www.amnestyusa.org

Amnesty International (AI) is an international nongovernmental organization that was formed in London in 1961 to attract attention to human rights abuses and war crimes perpetrated by governments against their people. AI was awarded the 1977 Nobel Peace Prize for its campaign against torture and often works to help the ICC with its investigations into genocide and other war crimes. It boasts a network of 2.2 million supporters, activists, and volunteers in more than 150 countries. AI publishes *Amnesty International Magazine*, which includes in-depth stories on human rights abuses and topics relevant to Amnesty International's mission. It also publishes a yearly report on the state of human rights all over the world.

Center for Constitutional Rights (CCR)
666 Broadway, 7th Floor, New York, NY   10012
(212) 614-6464
Web site: http://ccrjustice.org

Founded in 1966, the Center for Constitutional Rights (CCR) is a nonprofit legal and educational organization committed to advancing and protecting the rights guaranteed by the U.S. Constitution. CCR strives to use the law as "a positive force for social change." It does this through litigation that works to empower poor communities and by engaging and advocating for communities with limited access to legal resources. It publishes an annual report, numerous fact sheets on particular legal issues, and a quarterly e-newsletter that explores topics related to constitutional law and war crimes. On its Web site, it also offers access to reports and publications including *Current Conditions of Confinement at Guantánamo* and the *Guantánamo Global Justice Initiative News Briefing*, a monthly e-newsletter on the state of the fight to close the U.S. detention center in Cuba.

Council on Foreign Relations (CFR)
1777 F Street NW, Washington, DC   20006
(202) 509-8400 • fax: (202) 509-8490
e-mail: communications@cfr.org
Web site: www.cfr.org

The Council on Foreign Relations (CFR) is an independent, nonpartisan think tank and publisher. It is also a membership organization that works to be an invaluable resource for its members, politicians, government officials, business executives, media, students, and other interested people who are investigating U.S. national security policy and world events. CFR scholars publish articles, reports, in-depth studies, and books that analyze foreign policy issues and recommend policies to address world and national problems. CFR publishes *Foreign Affairs*, a journal focusing on international affairs and U.S. foreign policy. The CFR's Web site provides access to interviews, speeches, op-eds, reports, policy briefings, fact sheets, audio, transcripts, and video on a range of foreign security issues.

Genocide Intervention Network

1200 Eighteenth Street NW, Suite 320, Washington, DC   20036
(202) 559-7405 • fax: (202) 559-7410
e-mail: info@genocideintervention.net
Web site: www.genocideintervention.net

The Genocide Intervention Network was established in 2005 to mobilize citizens, leaders, and businesses against genocide around the world and to hold government leaders accountable for their passivity in the face of mass genocide and rape. The organization works closely with policy experts, world leaders, and social activists to fight against genocide and alert the public to situations occurring all over the world that merit attention and intervention, such as the mass killings in Burma, Darfur, and the Democratic Republic of the Congo. On its Web site, it publishes a blog and an e-newsletter, as well as news, updates on areas of interest, policy initiatives, and reports on pertinent subjects.

Global Centre for the Responsibility to Protect

365 Fifth Avenue, Suite 5203, New York, NY   10016-4309
(212) 817-2104 • fax: (212) 817-1565
e-mail: info@globalr2p.org
Web site: http://globalr2p.org

The Global Centre for the Responsibility to Protect is an organization dedicated to implementing the Responsibility to Protect doctrine in cases of genocide and mass rape. It advocates for further understanding of and support for the doctrine; formulates strategies to implement the doctrine and help nations fight against mass atrocities; and engages with nongovernmental organizations, governments, and regional groups that seek to promote and enforce the doctrine. The Global Centre's Web site offers access to a variety of speeches, seminar transcripts, conference papers, in-depth studies, and fact sheets on the fight to stop mass atrocities in areas such as Darfur, Burma, and the Democratic Republic of the Congo.

International Court of Justice (ICJ)

Peace Palace, Carnegieplein 2, The Hague   2517 KJ
   The Netherlands
(+31) (0)70 302 23 23 • fax: (+31) (0)70 364 99 28
Web site: www.icj-cij.org

Commonly referred to as the World Court, the International Court of Justice (ICJ) is the primary judicial institution of the United Nations (UN). The ICJ has a panel of fifteen judges that works to settle legal disputes submitted by member states and provides legal opinions to governmental agencies and the UN General Assembly. While the ICJ works on a wide range of disputes, the ICC focuses on cases dealing with crimes against humanity. A catalogue of publications is available on the ICJ's Web site, including legal opinions, briefs, advisory opinions, pleadings, and other legal documents accessible to the public.

International Criminal Court (ICC)

PO Box 19519, The Hague   2500 CM
   The Netherlands
(+31) (0)70 515 8515 • fax: (+31) (0)70 515 8555
Web site: www.icc-cpi.int

The International Criminal Court (ICC) is a permanent and independent international criminal court established to investigate and adjudicate cases of war crimes, genocide, and crimes against humanity in the international community. Established in 2002, the ICC is composed of 110 member states that have ratified the Rome Statute, the court's founding treaty. To date, the United States has not ratified the Rome Statute and therefore is not a member. The ICC was formed to exercise jurisdiction only in cases where the accused is a national leader and the government is unwilling or unable to prosecute or in cases referred to the court by the United Nations. The ICC has focused its efforts in four main investigations: Northern Uganda, the Democratic Republic of the Congo, the Central African Republic, and Darfur. The ICC's Web site is a useful resource for information on the court and international law pertaining to genocide, war crimes, and crimes against humanity as well as the current cases under investigation.

The R2P Coalition
c/o General Welfare Group LLC, 611 Enterprise Drive
Oak Brook, IL   60523
(630) 573-4403 • fax: (630) 573-0652
e-mail: info@R2Pcoalition.org
Web site: http://r2pcoalition.org

The R2P Coalition was founded to advocate for the Responsibility to Protect doctrine in the United States with political leaders and to be a persuasive voice in the fight to convince the United States to join the ICC. Ultimately, the R2P Coalition works to empower the United Nations and the ICC with an International Marshals Service, or standing police force, to allow the ICC to enforce international law. To this end, it has published a range of commentary, reports, fact sheets, and in-depth studies underscoring the need for international intervention in mass atrocities around the world in troubled areas including Darfur and the Democratic Republic of the Congo. The R2P Coalition also sponsors seminars, panel discussions, and other activities, all of which are listed on its Web site.

U.S. Department of State
2201 C Street NW, Washington, DC   20520
(202) 647-4000
Web site: www.state.gov

Established in 1789, the U.S. Department of State is a federal executive department in charge of diplomacy with other nations and is responsible for implementing the foreign policy of the United States. The State Department is led by the secretary of state, who is a member of the cabinet and the president's principal foreign policy advisor. In matters of war crimes and crimes against humanity, the State Department would be fully engaged in diplomatic efforts to bring perpetrators to justice and in facilitating humanitarian assistance across the globe. On the State Department's Web site, interested readers can access video, speech transcripts, press briefings, fact sheets, reports, congressional testimony, and indepth studies on American foreign policy issues.

Bibliography of Books

Tim Allen

Trial Justice: The International Criminal Court and the Lord's Resistance Army. New York: Palgrave Macmillan, 2006.

Roberto Bellelli

International Criminal Justice: Law and Practice from the Rome Statute to Its Review. Burlington, VT: Ashgate, 2010.

Christine Byron

War Crimes and Crimes Against Humanity in the Rome Statute of the International Criminal Court. New York: Palgrave Macmillan, 2009.

Pratap Chatterjee

Halliburton's Army: How a Well-Connected Texas Oil Company Revolutionized the Way America Makes War. New York: Nation Books, 2009.

Daniel Chirot and Clark McCauley

Why Not Kill Them All? The Logic and Prevention of Mass Political Murder. Princeton, NJ: Princeton University Press, 2006.

Barbara Coloroso

Extraordinary Evil: A Short Walk to Genocide. New York: Nation Books, 2007.

James Dawes

That the World May Know: Bearing Witness to Atrocity. Cambridge, MA: Harvard University Press, 2007.

Mark S. Ellis and Richard J. Goldstone, eds.
The International Criminal Court: Challenges to Achieving Justice and Accountability in the 21st Century. New York: International Debate Education Association, 2008.

Jennifer Elsea
International Criminal Court: Overview and Selected Legal Issues. Hauppauge, NY: Nova Science Publishers, 2006.

Helen Fein
Human Rights and Wrongs: Slavery, Terror, Genocide. Boulder, CO: Paradigm Publishers, 2007.

Lee Feinstein and Tod Lindberg
Means to an End: U.S. Interest in the International Criminal Court. Washington, DC: Brookings Institution Press, 2009.

Jolyon Ford
Bringing Fairness to International Justice: A Handbook on the International Criminal Court for Defence Lawyers in Africa. Tshwane, South Africa: Institute for Security Studies, 2009.

T. Marcus Funk
Victims' Rights and Advocacy at the International Criminal Court. New York: Oxford University Press, 2010.

Marlies Glasius
The International Criminal Court: A Global Civil Society Achievement. New York: Routledge, 2006.

David A.
Hamburg

Preventing Genocide: Practical Steps Toward Early Detection and Effective Action. Boulder, CO: Paradigm Publishers, 2010.

Joanna
Harrington,
Michael Milde,
and Richard
Vernon, eds.

Bringing Power to Justice? The Prospects of the International Criminal Court. Montreal, Quebec, Canada: McGill-Queen's University Press, 2006.

Ben Kiernan

Blood and Soil: A World History of Genocide and Extermination from Sparta to Darfur. New Haven, CT: Yale University Press, 2007.

Eve La Haye

War Crimes in Internal Armed Conflicts. New York: Cambridge University Press, 2008.

Peter Maguire

Law and War: International Law and American History. New York: Columbia University Press, 2010.

Harry P. Milton,
ed.

International Criminal Court: Policy, Status, and Overview. New York: Nova Science, 2009.

Kingsley Chiedu
Moghalu

Global Justice: The Politics of War Crimes Trials. Westport, CT: Praeger Security International, 2006.

Erna Paris

The Sun Climbs Slow: The International Criminal Court and the Search for Justice. New York: Seven Stories Press, 2009.

John T. Parry — *Understanding Torture: Law, Violence, and Political Identity.* Ann Arbor, MI: University of Michigan Press, 2010.

Jason Ralph — *Defending the Society of States: Why America Opposes the International Criminal Court and Its Vision of World Society.* New York: Oxford University Press, 2007.

Steven C. Roach, ed. — *Governance, Order, and the International Criminal Court: Between Realpolitik and a Cosmopolitan Court.* New York: Oxford University Press, 2009.

Philippe Sands — *Torture Team: Rumsfeld's Memo and the Betrayal of American Values.* New York: Palgrave Macmillan, 2008.

Jeremy Scahill — *Blackwater: The Rise of the World's Most Powerful Mercenary Army.* New York: Nation Books, 2007.

Suzanne Simons — *Master of War: Blackwater USA's Erik Prince and the Business of War.* New York: Collins, 2009.

Michael J. Struett — *The Politics of Constructing the International Criminal Court: NGOs, Discourse, and Agency.* New York: Palgrave Macmillan, 2008.

Otto Triffterer, ed. — *Commentary on the Rome Statute of the International Criminal Court.* Portland, OR: Hart, 2008.

Index

A

Abdul-Mahdi, Adil, 34
Abdulmutallab, Umar Farouk, 21
Abu Ghraib, 30–31, 39, 104
Aegis Defense Services, 33
Afghanistan, PSCs in, 31–32
African Union/United Nations
  Hybrid Operation in Darfur
  (UNAMID), 120, 173
Ahani, Ali, 15
Ahmadinejad, Mahmoud, 14–16
Ahmed, Abdul, 111
AI (Amnesty International), 67,
  157, 196
Al-Bashir, Omar Hassan Ahmad,
  133, 155, 167–169, 175
Al-Maliki, Nouri, 62
Al-Marri, Ali, 26, 28
Al-Shirbi, Ghassan Abdallah
  Ghazi, 111
Al Qaeda
  captured terrorists, 21, 111
  as criminals, 48–49
  as enemy combatants, 23–24
  legal protection, 107–108
  Somalia, 49–50
  undeserved status, 27
  U.S. incarceration, 107–113
Al Quds, 43
American Civil Liberties Union
  (ACLU), 55, 109
American Non-Governmental Or-
  ganizations Coalition for the
  International Criminal Court
  (AMICC), 195–165

American Service-Members' Pro-
  tection Act, 125, 137
American Society of International
  Law, 195
AMICC. *See* American Non-
  Governmental Organizations
  Coalition for the International
  Criminal Court
Amnesty International (AI), 67,
  157, 196
Amnesty International Magazine,
  196
Annan, Kofi, 15
Arab League, 158, 169
Article 98 agreements, 131, 146
Ashcroft, John, 39
ASIL. *See* American Society of
  International Law
ASIL Insights (journal), 195
ASIL Newsletter, 195
Askin, Kelly, 63
Associated Press (news
  organization), 184

B

Bahamas, 139
Barbados, 139
Barbary Pirates, 47
Bellinger, John B., 111, 119, 143–
  151
Bemba, Jean-Pierre, 59
Birns, Larry, 137–138
Blackwater Worldwide
  al-Maliki and, 42–43

Justice and Equality Movement (JEM), 154

K

Kellogg Brown & Root (KBR), 30
Kenya, 139–140
Kheiltash, Golzar, 137
Khomeini, Ayatollah, 14
King, Michael, 139
Kinsley, Michael, 21
Koh, Harold, 185–186
Kohler, Juliette Voinov, 75–86
Kosovo, 92
Kristof, Nicholas, 14–16
Kushayb, Ali, 155

L

L3 Communications Titan Group, 31
Law enforcement, 21–23
LCDH. See Central African Human Rights League
Legal force, 52–53
Lethal force, 52–53
Liberal-democratic states, 22–23
Lord's Resistance Army (LRA), 63, 133

M

Maersk Alabama (ship), 18–19, 47–48, 52–53
Major American Jewish Organizations, 15
Margaret Thatcher Center for Freedom, Heritage Foundation, 87
Martin, Ian, 157
Martin, Paul, 15

McCain, John, 92, 140
McCarthy, Andrew C., 183–190
Military Extraterritorial Jurisdiction Act (MEJA), 39
Military vs. contractors, 36–37
Mohammed, Khalid Sheikh, 111
Moonen, Andrew, 33–34
A More Secure World: Our Shared Responsibility (UN report), 73
Moreno-Ocampo, Luis, 59
MPRI company, 33
Muite, Paul, 139–140

N

Nation Institute, 51
National Institute for Public Policy, 41
National Review (periodical), 183
Nauru, 141–142
Navy SEALS, 44, 48, 52
Nethercutt Amendment, 137
New York Times (article), 14, 21
9/11 terrorist attacks, 21
Nisoor Square incident, 30, 32
Nobel Peace Prize, 196
Nowrojee, Binaifer, 65–70

O

OAS (Organization of American States), 139
Obama administration
    Goldstone Report, 165–166
    HRC and, 165
    ICC and, 116–117, 134
    Israeli-Palestinian conflict, 157, 165–166
    military force and, 22
    pirates treatment by, 48, 55–56

rule of law and, 184
Sudan, 168
transnationalism doctrine,
185–190
Obama, Barack, 92
OCODEFAD. *See* Organization for
Compassion and the Develop-
ment of Families in Distress
Open Society Initiative for East
Africa (OSIEA), 65
Open Society Institute, 88
Open Society Justice Initiative, 63
Organization for Compassion and
the Development of Families in
Distress (OCODEFAD), 60
Organization of American States
(OAS), 139

P

Pal, Amitabh, 135–142
Palacio, Alfredo, 138
Palestinian militants, 160
Palestinian-Israeli conflict, 156–
166
Passaro, David, 32, 39–40
Patassé, Ange-Félix, 59
Perdicaris, Ion, 47
Peres, Shimon, 14
Peru, 138
Phillips, Richard, 18, 47–48, 52–53
Pinochet, Augusto, 188
Pirates, piracy
attacks, 2006-2009, 48
controversy avoidance, 56–57
economic impact, 49–50
Geneva Convention and, 56
legal representation, 56–57
legal status, 48–49
Maersk Alabama, 18–19, 47–
48, 52–53

Obama administration and,
48, 55–56
prosecution, 54–55
rule of law, 55–56
threat hype, 54
warfare rules and, 48–50
Politics, 15–16
Blackwater Worldwide, 43
ICC, 131, 140–141, 148
PSCs and, 45
R2P doctrine, 85–86
terrorists, 112–113
war crimes, 184–185
Powell, Colin, 154–155, 173
Power of the state, 22–23
Private security contractors
(PSCs), 19, 29
Aegis Defense Services, 33
Afghanistan, 31–32
Blackwater Worldwide, 30,
33–34, 42–44
CACI International, 31
Centurion Group, 33
Control Risks Group, 33
crimes by, 30–31
CSA, 34
defined, 35
Department of State esti-
mates, 32
DOD estimates, 32
DynCorp International, 33
Erinys, 33
Human Rights First estimates,
32, 34
Human Rights First recom-
mendations, 38–39
Iraq, 30–44
L3 Communications Titan
Group, 31